AMAR

America's Strategic
Military Aircraft Reserve

JIM DUNN AND NICHOLAS A VERONICO

Front cover image: F/A-18A++ 163174/01, the commander's aircraft from the "Silver Eagles" of Marine Fighter Attack Squadron 115 (VMFA-115), was retired on January 30, 2019. (Jim Dunn)

Back cover image: In 1974, the Shah of Iran ordered 80 F-14A Tomcats for his country. The last of those Tomcats, F-14A BuNo. 160378, was held by the US and sent into storage at Davis-Monthan AFB, Arizona, when the Islamic Revolution forced the Shah to leave Iran. It would later be acquired by the Navy and entered service with the Naval Weapons Test Squadron at NAS Pt. Mugu as NF-14A 160378 (Modex 220). Ending its US Navy service on August 21, 2000, it is now in AMARG watching over a vast fleet of B-1s, B-52s, and C-5s. (Jim Dunn)

Contents page image: After first serving with the "Tomcats" of VMA-311, AV-8B 163877 (Modex 23) would go on to spend a number of years with the "Hawks" of VMAT-203 before being retired to AMARG in August 2020. The "Hawks" have been the USMC's Harrier training squadron for aircrew and maintenance personnel since receiving their first AV-8 in December 1983. (Jim Dunn)

Title page image: See page 36.

Dedication

To the legacy of aviation historians and photographers Rene J Francillion,
Peter B Lewis, and Frederick "Rick" Turner.

Acknowledgments

Recording the changes at AMARG over time requires a network of friends, aviation enthusiasts, and fellow writers and photographers located across the globe. Each has specialist knowledge and can provide the answer to many questions about particular aircraft. The authors are grateful to the following for their support on this and many other projects: Ian E Abbott, Jerry Anderson, Dana Backman, Jennifer Barnard, Roger Cain, Keith Charlot, Rich Dann, Ed Davies, Lou Drummond, John Dunlap, Corenthia K Fennell, Greg Forbes, Kevin Grantham, Michael Grove, Joe Gurney, Ted Holgerson, Jonathan Jackson, Dennis Jenkins, Richard Keane, Shawn Kirscht, Robert Kropp, Pat Kumashiro, William T Larkins, Del Laughery, Dave Leininger, Nate Leong, Jerry Liang, Michael H Marlow, Dale Messimer, Ken Miller, Donna Mrdjenovich, Paul Negri, Robert Nishimura, Dan O'Hara, Martin O'Leary, Michael O'Leary, Terry Pittman, Carl Porter, Taigh Ramey, Lee Scales, Doug Scroggins, Dorothy K Sherwood, Marc Sova, Ron Strong, Martyn Swann, Scott Thompson, James "Zip" Upham, Richard VanderMeulen, Betty Veronico, and Jerry Zacharuk. Thank you one and all.

Published by Key Books
An imprint of Key Publishing Ltd
PO Box 100
Stamford
Lincs PE19 1XQ

www.keypublishing.com

The right of Jim Dunn and Nicholas A Veronico to be identified as the authors of this book has been asserted in accordance with the Copyright, Designs and Patents Act 1988 Sections 77 and 78.

Typeset by SJmagic DESIGN SERVICES, India.

Contents

Foreword

By Colonel Patrick T Kumashiro (retired), USAF
Senior Advisor for F-35 Sustainment, Office of the Under Secretary of
Defense for Acquisition and Sustainment
309th AMARG Commander (2010–12)

The 309th Aerospace Maintenance and Regeneration Group (AMARG), aka "The USAF Boneyard" at Davis-Monthan AFB, Arizona, is clearly one of the most iconic and scenic vistas within the United States and the Department of Defense (DoD). Throughout its history, AMARG has been one of the most highly requested visits within the DoD, averaging a distinguished visitor tour every day of the year. During one such visit, the Indonesian Air Force Chief of Staff remarked in awe that seeing thousands of US military aircraft in storage is the sole reason why the United States of America remains the most powerful military in the world today, supported by the most prosperous global economy and prolific defense industrial base. This remark from a US ally was noteworthy and highlighted America's leadership in research, technology, and innovation. I quickly surmised that serving as AMARG's commander would be a tremendous honor and privilege.

When the authors reached out to me to discuss writing the foreword for this book to commemorate the 75th anniversary of AMARG, their request was both humbling and moving for me. Since I relinquished command of AMARG in 2012, I remember it as *the* best assignment in my 27-year USAF career. I have vivid memories of AMARG, including the thousands of military aircraft spanning more than 2,600 panoramic acres in Arizona and the extraordinary AMARG workforce that remains an enduring foundation of its remarkable success.

I had no idea that this assignment would be so memorable. I had previously viewed AMARG's mission as exclusively a storage and parts reclamation mission that was well-documented. However, I soon realized that AMARG and its workforce was the hidden gem supporting a critical and demanding depot maintenance overflow mission and parts reclamation capability generating hundreds of millions of dollars of annual savings for the DoD. Most importantly, AMARG regenerated aircraft in long-term storage to support critical operational requirements. This included resurrecting a B-52, nicknamed *Wise Guy*, that was stored in AMARG for more than ten years, to replace another B-52 that was permanently damaged during a fiery mishap in 2016. The complete overhaul of *Wise Guy* was a testament to the extraordinary skill sets of a determined USAF maintenance and logistics workforce and it was the second B-52 regenerated from AMARG. Additionally, AMARG supported and complied with recurring New START Treaty (NST) inspections, which included the first US inspection under NST protocol that furthered US national security objectives. These accomplishments would not have been possible without AMARG's remarkable workforce. AMARG's skilled artisans supported these demanding mission requirements in extreme temperatures and hazardous working conditions while avoiding Arizona's threatening wildlife that thrives within the facility's fence line. AMARG's success is the direct result of their dedication, professionalism, and agility, supporting operational requirements while preserving the history and memories for many military pilots and maintainers. These stories were emotionally moving, as many guests recounted the rich history of their experiences flying and maintaining these aircraft in support of our country.

Colonel Patrick T Kumashiro (USAF, retired) commanded the 309th AMARG from 2010 to 2012. He credits AMARG's success to the more than 800-strong workforce. (Courtesy of Patrick T Kumashiro)

In summary, I want to offer my sincere gratitude and thanks to the amazing AMARG workforce for their many successes that we had as an organization. I am fortunate to have witnessed their professionalism for two years. Congratulations on your 75th anniversary and your continued service to our country and the DoD!

Retired C-5 Galaxies sit at the 309th AMARG's Aircraft and Missile Storage and Maintenance Facility at Davis-Monthan AFB, Arizona, August 2, 2017. AMARG is the largest aircraft storage and preservation facility in the world. (US Force, photo by Staff Sgt Perry Aston)

Chapter 1

The Business of Aircraft Regeneration

S eeing one aircraft parked in the desert is an unusual sight, let alone seeing thousands in one place. Aircraft should fly, and although those in storage at the 309th Aerospace Maintenance and Regeneration Group (AMARG) typically do not, they do form an aircraft parts inventory, stored "on the wing" if you will, rather than on the shelves of a warehouse. Storage on the wing reduces costs and provides a quick, visual reference as to where parts are located. What most people don't know is that AMARG is so much more than a storage site for fixed- and rotary-wing aircraft, or a salvage station for parts to keep others flying.

The Air Force Sustainment Center (AFSC) is the parent of all three of the Air Force's depots (Ogden Air Logistics Complex, Oklahoma City Air Logistics Complex, and Warner-Robins Air Logistics Complex) as well as two supply chain wings and three air base wings under Air Force Materiel Command. AMARG is a subordinate organization to the Ogden Air Logistics Complex at Hill AFB, Utah, and a partner tenant of Davis-Monthan AFB, Tucson, Arizona. Davis-Monthan AFB encompasses more than 10,000 acres, of which AMARG occupies 2,600 acres, or a little more than one-quarter of the real estate. The region's hard-packed caliche soil, its temperate climate, minimal annual rainfall, and low humidity provide the perfect conditions for storing aircraft. Here, atmospheric-induced corrosion is only a small concern as opposed to aircraft stored in a salt-air environment. These attributes have earned AMARG the title of "America's National-level Airpower Reservoir."

Through the years, as AMARG's capabilities have grown, so has the facility's maintenance space with the addition of a 76,746sq ft high-bay hangar in 2015, and fighter-sized de-paint and paint facilities are projected for 2022. Currently, AMARG has 540,000sq ft of industrial workspace available for myriad tasks. What one does not see are giant warehouses for store parts. Storage on the wing moderates overhead costs by reducing warehouse facility requirements, maintenance, and utility costs. This also allows for a possible surge in storage and reclamation operations, making all parts and structural components available for reclamation.

AMARG's aircraft inventory ebbs and flows from year to year. Fiscal Year (FY) 1973 saw an all-time high of 6,080 aircraft in storage. AMARG currently stores approximately 3,200 aircraft, 5,900 engines of various models, and more than 340,000 pieces of aircraft production tooling. These assets are owned by more than 80 "customer" organizations from the US DoD (Army, Air Force, Marines, and Navy), the Department of Homeland Security (USCG, Customs and Border Protection), NASA, the Department of Agriculture (US Forest Service), the Smithsonian Institute, the National Science Foundation, and a number of Allied governments.

AMARG's mission encompasses five areas, from its well-known storage, reclamation, aircraft disposal, and regeneration activities to aircraft modification and overflow depot-level maintenance. In order to accomplish its mission, AMARG comprises the 309th Support Squadron (SPTS), the 576th Aircraft Maintenance and Regeneration Squadron (AMRS), and the 577th Commodities and Reclamation Squadron (CMRS).

KC-135Es and a single E-3A AWACS aircraft sit nose-to-tail at AMARG. The area's low humidity, infrequent rainfall, alkaline soil, and high altitude of 2,550ft above sea level are perfect conditions to store aircraft in a nearly rust- and corrosion-free environment. The KC-135E model aerial fueling tankers were originally introduced as KC-135A models but had their engines upgraded to TF-33-PW-102s when the USAF acquired a number of retired Boeing 707 commercial jetliners. All KC-135Es were retired in 2009 and were superseded by the CFM56-powered KC-135R. (USAF, photo by Staff Sgt Perry Aston)

The 309th Support Squadron provides maintenance and mission support, while the 576th AMRS is the facility's flight line squadron that performs the storage induction of arriving aircraft and staffs the various depot-level maintenance activities. The 577th CMRS is responsible for parts reclamation from stored aircraft and this unit's technicians prepare all aircraft departing by road. This is also the unit that surgically cuts stored strategic aircraft, such as the B-52 fleet, to comply with the New Strategic Arms Reduction Treaty, known as START.

The 309th Support Squadron provides maintenance and mission support to include A-10 wings, engine cowls, and F-16 landing gear overhauls. For a number of years, AMARG performed complete overhauls on A-10 wings. That line was shut down a few years ago as the A-10's future was debated in political circles. When the A-10's future became more secure, AMARG returned to the wing overhaul business by reclaiming wings from Warthogs stored in the desert. The work performed by the AMARG staff was a limited overhaul, or B-condition, which preserved the hours remaining on those sets of wings to be flown. These wing sets typically had about 1,000 flight hours left on them. To date, 27 sets of B-condition Warthog wings and main landing gear pods have been overhauled in the 309 Support Squadron's A-10 Wing Shop. Having completed nearly all of the limited-life wing overhauls, AMARG began a full overhaul program bringing wing sets up to A-condition status. The A-condition wings are rated for the full service life of 3,000 hours, and jets with A-condition wings have no maneuvering restrictions. The limited-life overhauls required 4,000–5,000 labor hours to complete, while A-condition overhauls can require up to 20,000 labor hours.

A-10C 79-0179 undergoes the parts reclamation process to keep other A-10 Thunderbolt IIs in the air. AMARG technicians are removing components from the cockpit of 79-0179, and, as can be seen, this Warthog has already given up its engines and most of its cowling. A-10C 79-0179's last assignment was with the 74th Fighter Squadron, 23rd Fighter Wing at Moody AFB, Georgia. The aircraft arrived for storage on January 24, 2014. (Jim Dunn)

AMARG's A-10 wing shop is giving many Warthogs an extended lease of life. Technicians are removing wings from A-10s parked in the desert and are overhauling them to a service life of 3,000 flight hours. These overhauls require 4,000–5,000 staff hours to complete. They are also performing higher level A-10 wing overhauls that take 20,000 staff hours. (Jim Dunn)

On February 22, 2016, a severe storm with golf-ball-sized hail struck Laughlin AFB, Texas. At the time 82 percent of the Beech T-1A Jayhawk aircraft of the 47th FTW were unsheltered and suffered damage that resulted in an 80 percent loss of T-1 pilot training capability. Owing to the large number of aircraft involved, it has taken years to return all of them to the fleet, with AMARG being one of the repair facilities taking part. Seen here on December 3, 2020, T-1A 93-0623 from the "Rio Lobos" of the 86th FTS, is being prepared for a functional check flight prior to returning to service at Laughlin AFB. This Jayhawk was the final T-1A delivered back to the fleet by AMARG. (Jim Dunn)

The 576th AMRS has several different production lines for the F-16 Fighting Falcon. The F-16 Depot Desert Speed Line project began installing multiple avionics modifications in FY 19, which was followed by the F-16 Post-Block Repair Program in October 2020. Technicians working on this program modify the F-16's center beam assembly, replace the inner and outer horizontal tail support beams, and inspect the aircraft's engine air inlet for corrosion. The F-16 depot overflow capability at AMARG also takes on priority assignments such as three Air National Guard F-16 Block 50 fighters heavily damaged in a weather-related event. Known as an Unscheduled Depot-Level Maintenance assignment, the aircraft arrived on trucks with many sub-assemblies in crates. AMARG technicians repaired and reassembled the jets, the last of which returned to its home unit in December 2020.

One of the major, ongoing F-16 activities at AMARG is the QF-16 Full-Scale Aerial Target Program. Col Jennifer Barnard, AMARG's commanding officer, said:

Through the years, AMARG has regenerated a variety of fighters for conversion into full-scale aerial targets. We have regenerated F-102s, F-100s, F-106s, F-4s, and now F-16s for conversion into drones used for weapons testing and targeting. In summer 2019, AMARG entered into a partnership with Boeing, where we now install F-16 "drone peculiar equipment" on site. First, we regenerate the F-16s for the program office, and then we install the drone peculiar equipment under a public private partnership with Boeing.

To date, the QF-16 Full-Scale Aerial Target Program has completed the regeneration of 114 F-16s.

AMARG and Boeing have formed a commercial collaboration to convert F-16s for the QF-16 Full-Scale Aerial Target program. AMARG technicians remove the fighters from the desert and de-preserve them. The aircraft are then modified into QF-16 configuration on a joint AMARG/Boeing production line. Six Fighting Falcons can be undergoing the drone conversion process simultaneously. (Jim Dunn)

Depot-level maintenance is also performed on F-16s at AMARG under various programs. F-16C Block 30K 88-0399 was delivered to the Air Force on June 26, 1989. The aircraft is assigned to the 100th Fighter Squadron, 187th Fighter Wing of the Alabama Air National Guard based at Dannelly Field. Once this maintenance period is over, these F-16s will return to their operational units. (Jim Dunn)

Photographed on May 13, 2020, departing on its first flight in nearly seven years, QF-16C 85-1402 is the first drone conversion to be completed at the Boeing/309th AMARG facility located at Davis-Monthan AFB. Delivered to the 526th TFS at Ramstein AB, West Germany, in November 1986, F-16C 85-1402 would later serve with the 706th FS at NAS New Orleans, and the 457th FS at NAS Fort Worth before arriving at AMARG on September 26, 2013. This joint public and private production line at AMARG supplements the Boeing line at NAS Cecil Field, Florida, to fulfill the current order for more than 120 QF-16A/C aircraft. (Nate Leong)

In September 2017, AMARG earned the first Federal Aviation Administration (FAA) Military Repair Station qualification for the AFSC to repair ten of the 39 hail-damaged T-1A Jayhawk multi-engine trainers. Because the T-1A is a corporate jet modified for military use, its maintenance is required to be performed by an FAA repair station certified to work on the Jayhawk. Col Barnard said:

Our overhaul program was the most extensive maintenance those aircraft had ever undergone. They were built in 1990–91, and we knew we were in for a lot of structural repairs, but we ended up doing a lot of other work to the aircraft along the way. Every aircraft took multiple functional check flights and our team did an exceptional job addressing the issues and working through them. We look forward to potentially serving the future needs of the T-1As.

The 577th Commodities Reclamation Squadron is responsible for preservation and in-storage maintenance of all aircraft and production tooling items, demilitarization of weapons system components prior to and during disposal, as well as the packing and shipment for overground transportation of aircraft, production tooling, as well as reclaimed parts and structural components. The 577th also surgically cuts aircraft for special engineering projects, reclamation, transport, or treaty compliance. Col Barnard continued:

We also have three Production Support Operations, Engineering and Quality Assurance. Production Support Operations is also known as business operations. It is the primary focal point for interaction with our customers and is where our asset and financial management professionals work. Our advanced planning staff is located within this organization as well as our IT department that runs our automated business systems. The Engineering Directorate supports flight line and desert production as well as the facilities and plant equipment across AMARG. We also have a fantastic Quality Assurance (QA) team that technically belongs to our parent command at the Ogden Air Logistics Complex. QA keeps our maintenance quality high.

Storage, Regeneration, and Elimination

Once a service or agency decides to remove a specific aircraft from the fleet temporarily or have determined the retirement path of a weapons system, it is sent to AMARG for storage or disposal in accordance with service or agency directives or the National Defense Authorization Act. This is decided through a disposition plan.

The disposition plan dictates which of the five levels of preservation will be required once the aircraft arrives. Type 1000 denotes long-term storage where the aircraft should be maintained in an intact condition with the potential of being recalled to active service. Aircraft in this status are re-preserved every four years. Type 1500 storage is similar to type 1000, except that they are not re-preserved. Examples are when some agencies want aircraft preserved to type 1000 standards for better parts protection with no intent to return to service and when some aircraft cannot undergo the full represervation process such as C-5As, which AMARG's wash facility isn't large enough to handle. Type 2000 signifies aircraft stored for parts reclamation to yield as many components as possible. Removed parts are cleaned, inspected, packaged, and shipped to repair depots or units around the world. Type 3000 denotes an aircraft in flyable hold storage and is often applied to aircraft awaiting transfer to a foreign government or awaiting formal disposition. Type 4000 storage signifies an aircraft that completed reclamation and is ready to be recycled. While stored in Type 4000, a service or agency may have the option to transfer an aircraft through foreign military sales to a partner nation or through the General Services Administration to another service or agency (such as from the Navy to the USCG), conduct regeneration, or dispose of the aircraft.

A KC-10 Extender from the 305th and 514th Air Mobility Wing at Joint Base McGuire-Dix-Lakehurst, New Jersey, flew into AMARG on July 13, 2020. This is the first of three KC-10s that were sent to storage in 2020, making 56 Extenders in the active fleet. KC-10A 86-0036 was built on October 6, 1986, and wore the nose art *Peace Maker*. During its career, 86-0036 flew 33,022.2 hours and was the 50th of 60 KC-10As built for the US Air Force. The type will eventually be replaced by the Boeing KC-46A Pegasus. Arrival on the AMARG ramp, as seen here, is the first step in the storage and parts reclamation process. (USAF/AMARG)

On average, during the past five years, approximately 215 aircraft have arrived for storage each year, and in the same time frame, an average of 281 aircraft have departed annually. When an aircraft flies into AMARG for storage, it lands on the base's runway and then taxies to the AMARG arrivals ramp. Once the paperwork has been completed, all armament is removed and life support technicians make the ejection seats safe. A green cross is spray painted on the port side, near the nose of the aircraft, to let staff know the aircraft is safe to work on and around. The aircraft's serial number and storage type are spray painted in black in the same vicinity.

Making the aircraft safe is followed by an inventory of the aircraft and its contents. This is followed by a detailed inspection of the aircraft. Then the hydraulic and fuel systems are serviced and the aircraft is thoroughly washed and sprayed with a corrosion inhibitor. Next it is towed to the desert where all openings are sealed. Openings on the upper sides of the aircraft are taped, leaving certain areas on the lower portion open, along with vent tubes to allow for air circulation. Engine inlets and exhausts have various amounts of desiccant inserted, to ensure any moisture is absorbed, and are then covered. Immediately afterward, the first of two coats of protective Spraylat is applied.

Spraylat is applied as an undercoat and a protective top coat. The undercoat of the protective Spraylat is black. This black layer acts as a sealant on the aircraft making it watertight. The top layer of Spraylat is white. This white layer bonds with the black undercoat creating a thermal barrier that reflects the sun's rays. Together, these two layers enable the aircraft's interior to maintain a temperature within 15 to 20 degrees of the outside air temperature.

The Engineering Directorate, working closely with preservation subject matter experts from the 577 CMRS' Logistics Services Flight, is developing a new, alternate protective coating, which is blue and provides the same level of protection necessary to keep moisture and animals out.

"In mid-2016, an H-60 was one of the first platforms to undergo preservation with the new blue, strippable preservation coating and white ceramic blend top coat, called Super Therm," said John

KC-130T US Navy Bureau of Aeronautics serial number (known as "BuNo.") 165353 is parked in the flush farm shortly after its arrival on November 24, 2020. This aircraft joined Marine Aerial Refueler Transport Squadron 352 (VMGR-352) in January 1996, and served for more than 14 years. While at the flush farm, all fuel systems are drained and the fluids captured and recycled for use in other aircraft. Preservative oils are then forced through the system and drained, also to be used again. This light coating of oil inhibits corrosion. (Jim Dunn)

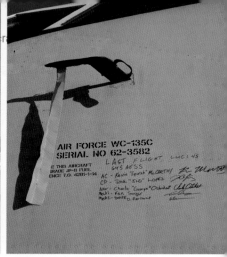

Above left, above right and below: **The mission it performed is called Constant Phoenix; the collection of air samples to determine if a nuclear event has occurred and who originated it. However, to the crews of WC-135C 62-3582 it was known as "Lucifer's Chariot" for the evil habit it had of stranding them in some less than pleasant locations around the world. On November 30, 2020, members of the 45th Reconnaissance Squadron at Offutt AFB, Nebraska, "signed off" on Lucifer's Chariot and dispatched it to the Arizona Desert with 56 years and 29,680 flight hours in its logbook. (Nicholas A Veronico)**

Dunlap, director of the Naval Supply Systems Command, Weapon Systems Support, Field Support Office, which manages all Navy aircraft at AMARG. Super Therm is a ceramic, water-based, heat reflective insulation paint. "The Super Therm material has ceramic beads in it that provide even more heat reflectivity than the Spraylat we currently use. This H-60 was withdrawn from storage after three and a half years and the test material was peeled and removed to allow for an inspection of the skin." On June 23, 2020, the same helicopter was resealed with the latest formulation of the blue strippable coating to continue its evaluation for future use. In addition, a side-by-side test of two P-3s is under way to enable a direct comparison between Spraylat and Super Therm. Dunlap continued:

After the aircraft is inducted into storage, there's an initial inspection of the preservation material at the 90-day mark, and then it goes into a 180-day cycle. The airplanes are inspected at 90 days and then 180 days after preservation. During these inspections, technicians make sure the aircraft remains securely tied down, that tires are at the correct inflation levels, and that the Spraylat material is not deteriorating in any way. That cycle is for Type 1000. Type 2000 level preservation is also entered into the 90/180-day

A new, experimental undercoating known as "Blue Super Therm" is being tested on a number of US Navy aircraft in storage at AMARG including EP-3E BuNo. 156514. This Orion was delivered on December 11, 1970, to VP-47 at Moffett Field, California. It subsequently served with VP-31, also at Moffett Field, followed by a short, one-year assignment to VP-19, before returning to VP-31. The aircraft was then modified to EP-3E Aries II configuration at the Naval Aviation Depot, Jacksonville, Florida. In September 1997, the aircraft was assigned to VQ-1 where it would fly until its career ended. The aircraft was flown to AMARG for storage arriving on April 26, 2016. The Blue Super Therm has been applied during one of the aircraft's represervation periods. (Jim Dunn)

inspection cycle, and repairs are made to the preservation coating throughout the aircraft's time in storage. The Navy uses Type 2000 level storage to help reduce foreign military sales (FMS) customer's cost when an aircraft is identified as a possible FMS candidate. We also use Type 2000 level storage to protect aircraft parts for aircraft being stored for reclamation, or aircraft being identified for eventual museum transfer.

Along with new materials, new aircraft types are arriving for storage. Recently, a pair of Northrop Grumman MQ-8B Fire Scout drone helicopters were sent to AMARG for storage. The drones arrived on June 30 and July 1, 2020, from Helicopter Sea Combat Wing Pacific at NAS Point Mugu, California. Built with extensive use of composites, nearly the entire front of the craft had to be sealed to protect its radome and access panels from exposure to the elements. In addition to the MQ-8Bs, 66 General Atomics MQ-1B Predator drones arrived for storage in fall 2018 and spring 2019, as the Air Force upgraded to the MQ-1C. The B-model Predators will yield parts to keep others flying and will eventually be recycled.

Supplying parts to the fleet from stored aircraft is a long-time aviation industry practice. For AMARG, the aircraft's owning agency or its program office determines which specific aircraft and what configuration and level of assembly will be reclaimed. Agencies may use a "programmed" approach to reclamation where parts from a fleet of aircraft, B-1s or B-52s for example, may be reclaimed from pre-identified aircraft. This pre-planned reclamation strategy may generate savings by avoiding removal costs in the future. Most parts are reclaimed via a "priority" approach to fill demands that cannot be supported with new or repaired parts in time to meet customer needs. This approach is used to meet

Someday this desert may become the final destination for a fleet of drone aircraft, but for now the population of drones at AMARG stands at 68. This number is made up of 66 MQ-1B Predator drones that are stored in containers after being retired by the USAF in 2018, and these two Northrop Grumman MQ-8B Fire Scouts shown shortly after arrival and in storage. Based on the Schweizer 333 and designed to operate from Frigates and Littoral Combat Ships, the MQ-8B can fly 110 nautical miles to locate, track, and designate targets. Fire Scout 168447 was retired on July 1, 2020, and 168448 on June 29, 2020. (USAF/AMARG and Nicholas A Veronico)

immediate mission requirements and does not generate savings. For both approaches, the part is inspected, tagged, packed, and shipped per guidance from the supply chain and program offices on the reclamation request. Once the reclaimed item reaches the shipment destination, it is entered into the supply chain inventory for either repair or direct customer use. In FY 20, 6,483 aircraft parts were reclaimed that originally cost the US government $363 million.

Aircraft leave AMARG when they have had all usable parts reclaimed, when they are regenerated and returned to their respective service or given to a new agency, sold to a friendly foreign government, preserved in a museum, or are ready to be recycled. Estimates are that more than 25 percent of all aircraft stored at AMARG have flown out to be operated again in some manner.

Certainly the highest profile aircraft regenerated by AMARG in recent years are two B-52H Stratofortress strategic bombers that have been returned to service in recent months. Both bombers had flown with the 5th Bomb Wing at Minot AFB, North Dakota, before they were sent to AMARG for storage; B-52H 60-0034 *Wise Guy* landing on August 14, 2008, and 61-0007 *Ghost Rider* arriving on November 13, 2008. *Ghost Rider* was the first to be regenerated and returned to the fleet on February 13, 2015, when it flew to Barksdale AFB, Louisiana, to have systems transferred from B-52H 61-0049, which had been heavily damaged in a fire. *Wise Guy* was regenerated and delivered to Barksdale AFB on May 14, 2019. It took the team at AMARG four months to put the bomber back into flying condition. Interestingly, both *Ghost Rider* and *Wise Guy* were simultaneously at the Oklahoma City Air Logistics Complex, Tinker AFB in November 2020, undergoing programed depot-level maintenance. (Both Nicholas A Veronico)

Two recent examples of aircraft that have been regenerated are the B-52Hs 61-0007 *Ghost Rider* and 60-0034 *Wise Guy* that both sat in storage for nearly a decade having arrived in 2008. Both bombers returned to the Air Force's Global Strike Command and are today on active duty. Other aircraft are dismantled by AMARG technicians and trucked to their new operator, or to reassembly/overhaul locations, which is often done when helicopter or fighter aircraft are sold to Allied nations.

Foreign Military Sales has long played an important role in AMARG operations. After an aircraft has been in storage for a period of years, it may be sold through various FMS programs to a new operator. This KC-130T, BuNo. 163022, was accepted by the US Marine Corps and assigned to Marine Aerial Refueler Transport Squadron 234 (VMGR-234) in September 1985. It later served with VMGR-452 and US Navy squadron VR-64 and was retired to AMARG on April 28, 2015. Sold to the Philippine Air Force, 163022 is seen taxiing out for a post-storage functional check flight on September 28, 2016. This Hercules arrived at Mactan Benito Ebuen AB, Cebu, Philippines, on October 9, 2016. It was given the Philippine Air Force serial number 5040. (USAF photo by Airman Nathan H Barbour)

This Polskie Zakłady Lotnicze (PZL-Mielec) M28 Skytruck departed AMARG on June 8, 2020, after nearly five years in storage. It was flown to Sierra Nevada Corporation of Centennial, Colorado, for refurbishment before beginning a new career with an FMS customer. Former USAF C-145A Combat Coyote 11-0326, N362DD, was one of 16 Skytrucks serving with Air Force Special Operations Command and was assigned to the 6th Special Operations Squadron (SOS) at Duke Field, Florida. These aircraft were used to train, assess, and prepare foreign air forces in techniques associated with military aircraft operations. (Jim Dunn)

Another important aspect of aircraft regeneration is to provide aircraft to museums, giving the public the opportunity to see restored examples of combat aircraft up close. General Dynamics F-16A Block 15 Fighting Falcon, serial number 80-0543, was delivered to the US Air Force on November 30, 1981, and was sent overseas to serve with the 313th TFS at Hahn AB, Germany, the following month. In December 1986, this F-16 was rotated stateside to serve with the 307th TFS at Homestead AFB, Florida. Converted to the ADF role in the late 1980s, the aircraft was next assigned to the 194th FIS (later the 194th Fighter Squadron), part of the 144th Fighter Wing of the California Air National Guard at Fresno. F-16A 80-0543 served until October 20, 1994, when it was flown to storage at AMARG. The fighter was transferred to the Air Force Museum's inventory and on January 28, 2016, assigned to the Castle Air Museum, Atwater, California. This Fighting Falcon arrived at the museum by truck on February 29, 2016. It has since been refurbished and placed on display with the museum's other 72 aircraft. (USAF/AMARG)

Those aircraft that have had all useful parts regenerated are scrapped. Some scrapping is done on site. However, most smaller aircraft are loaded onto trailers and driven from AMARG to the metal recyclers' yards adjacent to the air base. Large aircraft not scrapped on base are cut into a transportable size and trucked off base. Once at the recycler's facility, aircraft are shredded and the scrapper must certify that the aircraft has been destroyed. By law, the shredded pieces of aircraft can be no larger than 4 inches squared. A portion of the scrap value is returned to the US Treasury.

The last option for an aircraft to leave AMARG comes if it has been designated for preservation. This is often reserved for significant, history-making aircraft. Museums can request such aircraft by contacting the military services' national aviation museum. Communities, educational institutions, and certain veterans' groups can also acquire aircraft for display through the US General Services Administration. In both cases, receiving institutions must bear all the costs associated with disassembly, transportation, and restoration of these aircraft.

Looking to the Future

As the services transition to new aircraft types, certain fleets will be eliminated from the AMARG inventory. The Navy is sundowning a number of types and one of those facing the scrapper's torch is the North American Aviation T-2B and T-2C Buckeye jet trainer. Dunlap commented:

We were planning to eliminate the T-2, but at the last minute we found out that the missile test facility at Point Mugu, California, needed the Buckeye's engines. They came and got all of them for the target drones they fly there. When the target is done flying, it is recovered out of the water and that leads to a lot of corrosion issues. So they decided that they wanted to come to AMARG and get the J85s out of the Buckeyes. We had to delay our disposal of that type until they could remove all of the engines, but we're holding ten T-2s in reserve for the Greek government, which is still flying them. And then there's the P-3s. There are so many countries still flying P-3s that we're only rightsizing the fleet here. Almost every operator is, or will soon be, flying P-3Cs, so we're culling our inventory down to just C-models that have the same equipment our customers are flying. I would imagine that we're going to have P-3s in storage for another 25 years. We are going to eliminate all of the S-3s and we're demilitarizing some H-53s right now. We're pulling parts out of EA-6Bs and when we're done, we're going to dispose of those as well.

"What impresses me most about AMARG is the caliber of the team here," said Col Barnard:

Almost 800 people work here and take care of nearly 3,200 aircraft – not counting all the aircraft that pass through for modification and repair. Our workforce's diverse skill set enables us to tackle any variety of complex projects. We have people that spent time in each of the military services. Some of them came straight from civil aviation and some of them from the community. Yet, our team comes together and works really well capitalizing on one another's perspective and strengths.

AMARG's staff are looking to the future when the levels of legacy aircraft in storage may decline and be replaced by types with greater percentages of composite structures or possibly fifth generation fighters As this change occurs, and as the services continue to operate aircraft types to their limits, it is likely that AMARG's mission and its skilled workforce will transition to more modification and overhaul work. In the interim, AMARG continues its mission as a strategic aircraft reserve supporting the warfighting capabilities of the US Air Force, Army, USCG, Navy, and Marines.

When individual aircraft have been picked clean and are no longer of any value to the fleet, they are sold for scrap. A number of metal recyclers have taken up residence along AMARG's southeastern fence line, enabling contractors to tow or transport aircraft to its facilities for conversion into recyclables. Leading the way is EA-6B BuNo. 158040, which last flew with Electronic Attack Squadron One Three One (VAQ-131) and arrived at AMARG on September 30, 2009, followed by 163892, a veteran with Marine Tactical Electronic Warfare Squadron Two (VMAQ-2), which flew into storage on November 2, 2009. These two EA-6Bs, seen on December 5, 2020, will be shredded into pieces no larger than 4 inches squared. (Nicholas A Veronico)

B-1B 85-0092 *Apocalypse,* was the tenth Lancer to arrive at AMARG for storage, landing on September 17, 2002. In a partnership between the US Air Force and the National Institute for Aviation Research at Wichita State University, Kansas, this B-1B will be used to make a "digital twin." The digital twin will reveal structural failures or damage, and the data collected will be matched with maintenance and inspection data from the aircraft's service life. Computer simulations will also assist in parts prototyping where components can be test fitted without cutting the aircraft's structure. Knowledge gained from this analysis will aid in future warfighting aircraft design. (USAF/AMARG; nose art: Nicholas A Veronico)

After 18 years sitting in desert storage, this is what an F-16 Fighting Falcon looks like when its protective coating is removed for inspection. Well-traveled F-16A Block 15, serial number 80-0602, was in the first cadre of F-16s assigned to the 10th Tactical Fighter Squadron (TFS) at Hahn AB, West Germany, in mid-1982. It stayed in Europe until May 1986, when it joined the 182nd TFS of the Texas ANG at Kelly AFB. Converted to an Air Defense Fighter (ADF) it took up the role of an interceptor with the 186th Fighter Interceptor Squadron (FIS) of the Montana ANG in April 1992. This was a short stay as it would join its final unit, the 198th Fighter Squadron (FS) of the Puerto Rico ANG, in October 1992. It was retired to AMARG on March 23, 1998, and is now back in storage with a new protective coating. (Jim Dunn, Nicholas A Veronico)

Once considered the most reliable of its tanker/transport fleet, the USAF's McDonnell Douglas KC-10A Extender is now paying the toll for many long, hard missions supporting the War on Terror. With the Boeing KC-46 slowly beginning to enter service, the first three of the 59 KC-10As were retired in the summer of 2020 marking the arrival of this new type at AMARG. Two of the aircraft, KC-10A 86-0036 and 87-0120, came from the 305th AMW at Joint Base McGuire-Dix-Lakehurst, New Jersey, while KC-10A 83-0077 was with the 60th AMW at Travis AFB, California. (Jim Dunn)

Above left and above right: In addition to aircraft parked in rows, AMARG also stores 340,000 pieces of aircraft production tooling, aircraft sub-assemblies like the B-52 cruise missile pylons shown here, and engines of various types and in differing conditions. AMARG is currently storing more than 5,900 engines including high-bypass engines like the TF39 (pictured right) that powered the C-5A and B, and the TF33 (pictured left) that power the B-52. (Engines: Ron Strong; Pylons: Nicholas A Veronico)

Political pressure led the USAF to order 38 Alenia C-27J Spartans it did not want, with the end result being only 21 delivered and several of those being flown directly to storage at AMARG. The saga would continue when the US Coast Guard (USCG) would obtain 14 of the Spartans and send seven of its HC-130H aircraft to the US Forest Service (USFS) in its failed attempt to use them for their own in-house firefighting program. Since they had been intended for ANG service, a few C-27s made it into operation with units of the Ohio and Mississippi ANG, with C-27J 09-27022 serving with the 186th AW at Meridian, Mississippi. The end result is that this Spartan now serves as USCG HC-27J 2713 at USCG Air Station Sacramento, which had to give up its HC-130H aircraft to the USFS. (In storage: Jim Dunn; In service: Roger Cain)

The Maintenance Shelter is where a lot of action happens at AMARG. Incoming aircraft are prepared for storage and those being regenerated for new operators are worked on here. This crop of F-16s is being prepared for the full-scale drone program. In the foreground is F-16C Block 25C 84-1223, which flew 44 missions in Operation *Desert Storm* with the 17th Tactical Fighter Squadron and was deployed to Operation *Iraqi Freedom* with the 111th Fighter Squadron. The aircraft arrived for storage on May 8, 2008. (Jim Dunn)

F-16s often leave AMARG on pallets. The aircraft can be shipped from the center to repair depots around the country, or when regenerating and flying an aircraft to a foreign military sales customer's home base is not an option. In addition to the fuselage on a skid, various boxes of components and the wings make up the shipment. (Jim Dunn)

75 Years Supporting America's Warfighting Capability

During World War Two, the United States built more than 300,000 aircraft for America and its Allies. The atomic bombing of Japan in fall 1945 effectively ended World War Two and simultaneously made thousands of military aircraft obsolete. Jet fighter aircraft were a reality, and this new technology would soon produce medium and intercontinental range jet bombers.

America's aviation arsenal of piston-powered fighters and bombers was soon to be replaced, and the aircraft of World War Two would meet their end at the scrapper's torch – their aluminum skin melted to feed post-war consumer demand for new cars and appliances. Yet, America needed a strategic aircraft reserve, where still-useful bombers and transports could be stored for future use.

Two strategic aircraft reserve bases were established, one at Pyote, Texas and the other adjacent to Davis-Monthan Army Air Field, Arizona. Pyote stored B-17s, B-29s, and light bombers such as the B-25 and A-26. In addition to the two storage facilities, six storage depots were formed at Hill AFB, Ogden, Utah; Tinker AFB, Oklahoma City, Oklahoma; Kelly AFB, San Antonio, Texas; Norton AFB, San Bernardino, California; McClellan AFB, Sacramento, California; and the Warner-Robbins Air Materiel Area, Warner, Georgia.

Operations at Davis-Monthan were managed by the 4105th AAF Base Unit (Aircraft Storage), a unit of the Second Air Force, beginning on April 1, 1946. The 4105th Base Unit had parked and preserved 690 B-29s and 241 C-47s by the end of the year.

A big change came in 1964, when the DoD consolidated all military storage and regeneration activities at Davis-Monthan AFB and changed the name of the unit to the Military Aircraft Storage and Disposition Center (MASDC). The unit's name was changed to the Aerospace Maintenance and Regeneration Center (AMARC) in 1985. In May 2007, the center's reporting structure changed, now reporting to the Ogden Air Logistics Center, Hill AFB, Utah, and with that came a name change to the AMARG.

Highlights of AMARG's 75 years of supporting the DoD include:

- In 1948, the Soviets blocked all access leading into Berlin, which led to the initiation of the Berlin Airlift. AMARG regenerated C-47s for the effort and provided parts support to keep the air bridge alive until the Soviets acquiesced.
- In 1950, North Korea invaded South Korea, starting the Korean War. AMARG regenerated B-29 bombers as well as C-47 Skytrains to aid the effort in stopping the spread of communism in the region.
- In 1962, during the Cuban Missile Crisis, AMARG shifted from reclaiming B-47 bombers to "stand-by to regenerate in case of war" when President Kennedy ordered the US Air Force on full alert when the threat of nuclear war was imminent.
- In 1964, there was an exchange of fire in the Gulf of Tonkin that escalated America's involvement in the Vietnam Conflict. AMARG again began regenerating C-47s that became the first gunships and A-1 Skyraiders. These aircraft pioneered search and rescue procedures for downed airmen during the conflict. Also regenerated for counter-insurgency operations were the B-26s and T-28s.
- AMARG has played a key role in the Strategic Arms Reduction Treaty by dismantling and destroying B-52 bombers. In the late 1980s, AMARG eliminated ground-launched cruise missiles in support of the Intermediate Nuclear Forces Treaty and began storing Titan IIs when Norton AFB, California closed.
- In the 1990s, when Iraq invaded Kuwait, AMARG provided F-4, F-15, F-16, A-10, C-141, F-111, and B-52 airpower parts/assets as part of Operations *Desert Shield* and *Desert Storm*.

- AMARG answered the call when the US Air Force needed to rapidly increase C-130 operations and the aircraft required wing changes because of heavy corrosion. In short order, AMARG began work on the C-130 Outer Wing Overhaul Project from July 2015 to October 2019.
- When a typhoon with tsunami-like effects ravaged the Philippines in 2013, the US State Department agreed to sell two KC-130Ts to that country, so that when future natural disasters happen, the Philippines would have transport aircraft to move rescue personnel, evacuate victims, and save lives.
- In 2015, the Air Force Global Strike Command needed an additional B-52 bomber to aid in the War on Terrorism and for nuclear deterrence. AMARG worked with an integrated Air Force team and regenerated B-52H 61-0006 *Ghost Rider*, that had been in storage for seven years. B-52H 60-0034 *Wise Guy* was subsequently regenerated and added to the fleet.
- When forest fires ravaged the western United States in 2013, Congress directed the USCG to transfer C-130 aircraft to the Forest Service and stand-up two USCG units to fly C-27s – a smaller, newer cargo aircraft. AMARG, working with the USCG, regenerated 13 C-27Js, allowing full operational capability nationwide.

The mission has, essentially, remained constant for 75 years, although the aircraft types and the technologies they represent have changed greatly. AMARG is looking to the future as its role within the Air Force's maintenance structure increases and its workforce and facilities are prepared for handling the next generation of aircraft.

Rare color photo of the Douglas XB-19 on the AMARG ramp with hundreds of B-29 Superfortresses in the background. In 1943, the experimental bomber was fitted with Allison V-3420-11 engines (two V-1710 engines with a common crankcase). The XB-19 last flew on August 17, 1946, and was scrapped in June 1949. (Courtesy of Pima Air and Space Museum)

Hundreds of cocooned B-29s are parked as far as the eye can see in the early months of 1950. Soon, three-quarters of these aircraft would be regenerated to support the air war over the Korean peninsula. (National Archives)

B-29 44-27297 *Bockscar*, named for its pilot Frederick C Bock, dropped the second atomic bomb of World War Two on August 9, 1945. Its target was the city of Nagasaki. *Bockscar* was stored in September 1946 and flew out to the National Museum of the US Air Force in September 1961. (Authors' Collection)

Chapter 2
Attack, Fighters, and MiG Killers

Intended to become the most advanced storm penetrating aircraft in the history of the National Science Foundation, A-10C 80-0212 never made it into this new battle. The combat veteran was loaned from the 354th FS at Davis-Monthan AFB and had been demilitarized and highly modified for its new role, before a series of events resulted in it instead being sent to AMARG on April 30, 2019. As of the end of 2020, it is the most recent retirement of an A-10 to AMARG, and the US Congress has imposed restrictions on the USAF regarding reductions in the A-10 fleet. (Jim Dunn)

Above, left and below: Since World War Two, the "Dogpatchers" of the 47th FS have adopted the famous American comic strip *Li'l Abner* and the humorous characters of "Dogpatch USA" as their squadron mascots. Flying the A-10 since 1980 in both a training and combat coded role, this Air Force Reserve Command (AFRC) Squadron is now based just across from AMARG on the active side of Davis-Monthan AFB. Seen in April 2004, when it hosted the Hawgsmoke gunnery meet in Alexandria, Louisiana, A-10C 79-0149 carries the image of General Bullmoose the capitalist tycoon of Dogpatch. After entering AMARG on April 19, 2013, General Bullmoose has been donating parts to keep other A-10s flying, but sadly, while the Dogpatchers of the 47th FS now wear the "DP" tail code on their jets, all the character images from *Li'l Abner* have been removed. (Jim Dunn)

An upgrade to eight Lockheed AC-130E gunships would produce the AC-130H Spectre. Five of these gunships, including AC-130H 69-6569, were deployed by the 16th SOS from Hurlburt Field, Florida, in September 1990 to support Operation *Desert Shield*. Over the next 25 years, the 16th SOS would fly thousands of combat sorties in Operations *Desert Storm*, *Enduring Freedom*, and *Iraqi Freedom,* to name just a few of the engagements its AC-130H gunships took part in. On May 27, 2015, AC-130H 69-6569 *Excalibur* would become the last of the AC-130H Spectre gunships to be retired and flown to AMARG. (Jim Dunn)

Above and left: In operational service from 1995 until August 2019, the AC-130U Spooky II was the third generation of gunships flown by the USAF. Equipped with a 25mm GAU-12/U 5-barrel rotary cannon, a 40mm L/60 Bofors cannon, and a 105mm M102 Howitzer, AC-130U 90-0167 *Intimidator* served with the "Ghostriders" of the 4th SOS at Hurlburt Field, Florida, until being retired on December 10, 2019. (Jim Dunn)

Below: Only 11 single-seat models of the Douglas A-4 Skyhawk remain in the inventory at AMARG. One of these is A-4F 155018 (Modex 27; written as 155018/27), a Vietnam combat veteran that last served as a Top Gun adversary aircraft. While assigned to the Ghostriders of VA-164 aboard the USS *Hancock* (CVA-19) on Yankee Station off the coast of North Vietnam, it flew bombing missions in support of Operations *Freedom Train* and *Linebacker I* in the spring of 1972. With an engine upgrade making it an A-4F Super Fox, it took on its final role with the "Bandits" of VF-126 as an adversary at NAS Miramar, California. Retired on March 28, 1994, its adversary paint scheme has now almost completely faded away. (Jim Dunn)

Above, right and below:
In November 2011, the Ministry of Defence in the United Kingdom undertook the controversial decision to sell its retired fleet of 72 Harriers, along with spares, for $180 million dollars to the United States. Arriving at AMARG in April 2012, the Harriers have been used to help maintain the USMC Harriers, scheduled to remain in service until their replacement by the F-35B. Stored with their wings and fuselages separated, there are currently 3 GR-7, 47 GR-9, and 8 TMK-12 aircraft on the AMARG inventory. (Jim Dunn)

A good indication that an aircraft type is nearing the end of its service is when examples from the training unit begin to be retired. A large parking area has been prepared to receive the USMC fleet of AV-8B Harriers as they are replaced by the Lockheed F-35B Lightning II. By December 2020, the first eight USMC AV-8Bs had taken up residence at AMARG, as seen here. From the "Hawks" of Marine Attack Training Squadron 203 (VMAT-203) at MCAS Cherry Point, North Carolina, AV-8B 163869 (Modex 26) arrived on July 28, and was followed soon after by 163877/23 on August 17, 2020. (Nicholas A Veronico)

Also known as "Vandy 1," the "Black Bunny" F-4 is probably the most recognizable of all the F-4 Phantoms. Flown by "The Evaluators" of Air Test and Evaluation Squadron Four (VX-4) based at NAS Point Mugu, California, this squadron carried on the rabbit head markings that dated back to 1953 and Marine squadron VMCJ-2. With stencils now provided by Playboy Enterprises to avoid legal conflict, F-4S 155539 is actually the second Black Bunny Phantom for VX-4. The first and best known was F-4J 153783 that was transferred to the RAF in August 1984 to become ZE351. For F-4S 155539 retirement would come on May 2, 1986, when a Black Bunny F-14 Tomcat took its place. In summer 2021, the "Black Bunny" will be transported to its new home at the Castle Air Museum in Atwater, California. (Nicholas A Veronico)

In the early 1970s, the Luftwaffe ordered 175 McDonnell F-4F Phantoms to replace its aging Lockheed F-104s. The United States was chosen as the location for aircrew training and the USAF "Silver Lobos" of the 20th TFTS at George AFB, California was its first base. Later it would move to Holloman AFB, New Mexico, where this training would continue until December 20, 2004. The aircraft remaining at that time became the final Phantoms to enter AMARG when they were flown there in early January 2005. These F-4Fs would then supply parts to other Luftwaffe Phantoms until their final retirement on June 29, 2013. (Jim Dunn)

Another resident of Display Row is this Century Series F-101B Voodoo, 57-0436, which last flew with the 136th FIS, New York ANG. The 136th FIS received its first F-101Bs in June 1971 and the following year became a component of the North American Air Defense Command (NORAD). The 136th was part of the 24-hours, 365-days-per-year defense of America's northern and Atlantic Ocean facing borders. The unit transitioned to the F-4C Phantom II in 1981, parking its Voodoos. This F-101B arrived on September 21, 1981, and is the last of its type in AMARG. (Nicholas A Veronico)

Now in its place of honor on Display Row, F-105G 63-8285 is the last Republic Thunderchief at AMARG. In 1968, while serving with the "Vampires" of the 44th TFS based at Korat RTAFB, Thailand, 63-8285 was dual capable in both the Wild Weasel and Commando Nail missions, the latter involving night radar bombing. Its active duty ended in 1980 with the "Black Knights" of the 561st TFS at George AFB, California, with it then being sent to Davis-Monthan AFB to enter the US Air Force Museum loan program. Displayed first at Davis-Monthan AFB, it would not enter the AMARG inventory until February 19, 2014, when it went on Display Row. (Jim Dunn)

On March 19, 1990, McDonnell Douglas F-15C, 81-0054, was in a flight of two Eagles flying from Elmendorf AFB to Galina, Alaska, when it was struck by a live AIM-9M Sidewinder missile. Both aircraft were practicing intercepting one another when one pilot, who thought he was firing a simulated missile, fired. The pilot in the target aircraft was warned the missile was hot and he began evasive maneuvers, pulling into the sun to blind the missile. The Sidewinder found its target, striking the rear of the Eagle. Extensive damage was done to the port engine, left horizontal stabilizer, and vertical tail, and although the pilot was able to land the jet, the resulting repair bill covered nearly $1 million in damage. A tail from another wrecked F-15 was used to repair the aircraft. F-15C 81-0054 last served with the 58th Fighter Squadron, 33rd Fighter Wing at Eglin AFB, Florida. The Eagle arrived at AMARG on September 8, 2009. (Nicholas A Veronico)

One of the most popular fighters of the modern era is the Grumman F-14 Tomcat. Today, five A models, two B models, and three D models, are all that remain in the AMARG inventory. Flying combat missions during *Desert Storm* while assigned to the "Tophatters" of VF-14 aboard the USS *John F Kennedy*, F-14B 162691/112 would end its service with the "Swordsmen" of VF-32 on September 21, 2005. Another combat veteran is F-14D 164602/213 that is displayed outside of the Navy office at AMARG. This Tomcat flew with the "Black Lions" of VF-213 aboard the USS *Carl Vinson* during Operation *Desert Fox* and later dropped the first bombs of Operation *Enduring Freedom*. Later, aboard the USS *Theodore Roosevelt,* it participated in Operation *Iraqi Freedom*. This third from last Tomcat built was retired on March 28, 2006. (Nicholas A Veronico and Jim Dunn)

Located on the east side of AMARG Area 27 is the last area before the final journey to the scrapper for these F-15s. All the F-15A/B/C/D models of the Eagle now in storage arrived between 2007 and 2010. A number of Eagles were retired early during this period because of an accident that disclosed structural problems in their upper longerons. Most of these Eagles came from ANG service, with a few being heavily used examples from the active-duty training units at Tyndall AFB, Florida. (Jim Dunn)

This view from August 2012 would look much different if seen today. Illustrating that AMARG undergoes constant changes in its areas, as well as its regeneration of aircraft, two of the F-16s seen here would find new duties with a foreign air force. Through the FMS program, Peace Bima-Sena II, both F-16C 85-1406 (Vermont) and 85-1447 ("EF" tail code), were sent to the Indonesian Air Force (TNIAU) where 85-1406 became TS 1640, and 85-1447 became TS 1643. Unfortunately for TS 1643, it was shortly thereafter damaged beyond repair in a take-off accident on April 16, 2015. (Nicholas A Veronico)

Right and below: F-15A 76-0084 sits in storage with its wings removed to keep another Eagle in the air. Its current state belies its significant contribution to aerospace history. In 1985, then-Major Wilbert "Doug" Pearson Jr (later Major General, USAF retired), a Vietnam combat pilot, was commander of the F-15 Anti-Satellite Combined Test Force at Edwards AFB, California. The culmination of the Combined Test Force was the September 13, 1985, flight when Pearson, flying at Mach 1.22 pulled back on the stick putting the Eagle into a 65-degree zoom climb. Reaching 38,100ft and decelerating to Mach 0.934, computers on board the Eagle calculated the firing solution and launched an 18ft long (5.49m), 20in diameter (50.8cm), three-stage ASM-135 missile that impacted the Solwind P78-1 satellite flying 345 miles above the earth.

In 2007, F-15A 76-0084, now known as *Celestial Eagle*, was assigned to Homestead Air Reserve Base and the 125th Fighter Wing, Florida, ANG. Pearson's son, Air Force Capt Todd Pearson, flew the aircraft on September 13, 2007, to commemorate the achievement. Three years later, on August 19, 2010, *Celestial Eagle* arrived at AMARG for storage. There is still hope that this aircraft can be preserved. (Nicholas A Veronico and USAF)

While a number of F-16s have already been set aside to become QF-16 drones, a larger number will have donated all their useful parts and eventually be designated for scrap. Now awaiting its end in Area 22 is F-16A 80-0523, which had last served in the 465th FS at Tinker AFB, Oklahoma, from 1989 until retirement on February 23, 1994. (Jim Dunn)

Overhauled F-16s await their turn to be converted to QF-16 full-scale target drones. AMARG and Boeing have partnered to open a second modification line to supplement the conversions done at Boeing's Cecil Field, Florida site. The first AMARG/Boeing-converted QF-16 was delivered to Tyndall AFB, Florida in June 2020. The Fighting Falcon leading the line is F-16C Block 30B 85-1544 that was delivered on March 31, 1987, and last flew with the 119th Fighter Squadron, New Jersey ANG. This aircraft arrived for storage on July 2, 2013. (Jim Dunn)

In 2016, Boeing was chosen to upgrade and extend the life of 30 F/A-18C Hornets, 23 of which would come from storage at AMARG. After eight years in the desert, F/A-18C 163767 is seen in its custom storage cover ready for shipment to the Boeing facility in Jacksonville, Florida. A veteran of the Gulf War with the "Stingers" of VFA-113 flying from the USS *Independence*, it would go on to serve a tour with the Marines "Lancers" of VMFA-212 before being retired to AMARG on October 21, 2008, after a final tour back in the Navy with the "Warhawks" of VFA-97. In 2020, the number of these Legacy Hornets to be upgraded to F/A-18C+ standards had been reduced to 19, with all the aircraft to be assigned to the "Cowboys" of Marine Reserve squadron VMFA-112 in Fort Worth, Texas. (Jim Dunn)

Not to be outdone when it comes to colorful markings on their commander's aircraft, the "Silver Eagles" of Marine Fighter Attack Squadron 115 (VMFA-115) demonstrate their talent on F/A-18A++ 163174/01. Current plans call for four USMC VMFA squadrons to convert from the Legacy Hornet to the F-35C for deployments with Navy carrier air wings (CVWs). The Silver Eagles are scheduled to be one of these squadrons, with conversion now planned for 2023. For F/A-18A++ 163174/01 its long active service career came to an end when it was flown to AMARG on January 30, 2019. (Jim Dunn)

Arriving on January 25, 2019, F/A-18B 161924/12 is one of only eight two-seat F/A-18Bs currently at AMARG and is also the oldest Legacy Hornet in storage there. As the flagship of the "Fighting Omars" of VFC-12 at NAS Oceana, Virginia, a Navy Reserve unit providing adversary support to East Coast-based squadrons, this Hornet featured a distinctive aggressor paint scheme known by the squadron's callsign as "Ambush." (Jim Dunn)

The US Navy Flight Demonstration Squadron, the Blue Angels, transitioned from the legacy F/A-18 Hornet, beginning in 2019, to the F/A-18 Super Hornet in preparation for the anticipated 2021 airshow season. The team had flown Legacy Hornets for 34 years and the transition was timed to coincide with the Blue Angels' 75th anniversary season. The new aircraft are Block 1, Lot 21-25 Super Hornets that are modified with an oil tank that is plumbed to vent into the aircraft's exhaust to produce smoke, inverted fuel pumps to enable extended inverted flight, and a spring on the control stick changing how the aircraft feels and enabling the pilots to fly such close formations.

Legacy F/A-18C Hornets number 5, BuNo. 163741, one of the solo aircraft, and Number 2, BuNo. 163462, flown in the diamond formation, both became Blue Angels aircraft for the 2018 season. More than 30 former Blue Angel F/A-18s are on public display around the country. (Nicholas A Veronico)

It is rare in the service history of an F/A-18 Hornet to find an assignment to an elite squadron such as the Blue Angels and rarer still to find one that had served with both the "Blues" and as an adversary at the famed Top Gun school. Beginning its career with the "Fist of the Fleet" VFA-25 and then the "Golden Dragons" of VFA-192, F/A-18C 163754 was chosen to receive a Sukhoi Blue paint scheme for its next assignment to the Naval Strike and Air Warfare Center at NAS Fallon, Nevada. Here it would be flown by some of the Navy's best pilots in air-to-air combat training against fleet aircrews and Top Gun students, before being assigned to the Blue Angels and serving in the 2015–16 season as "Blue Angel 1." After receiving depot-level maintenance, it was flown in for storage on November 6, 2020, by LCDR Ryan "NcNutty" McNulty. (Jim Dunn)

MiG Killers at AMARG

Parked among the storage rows are five fighters with aerial victories to their credit. One Air Force and two Navy F-4 Phantom IIs with victories in Vietnam, an F-14 that downed a Libyan MiG-23, as well as an F-15C with a kill in Operation *Desert Storm* are preserved at AMARG awaiting their final fate. Gone but not forgotten are a pair of F-15C MiG Killers, serial numbers 79-022 and -069, that recently left AMARG to be displayed for the public to see and to represent the conflicts in which they engaged.

Above: Parked on Display Row is F-4C 64-0699, a Phantom II that last flew with the 123rd FIS, 142nd Fighter Interceptor Group, based at Portland International Airport, Oregon. Capt Robert E Blake and 1st Lt S W George achieved an aerial victory in this Phantom early in the Vietnam War while assigned to the 555th TFS, 8th Tactical Fighter Wing, based at Udorn RTAB, Thailand. On April 23, 1966, they engaged a MiG-17 and brought it down with an AIM-7D Sidewinder missile. This Phantom arrived for storage on July 20, 1989, and was moved to the Davis-Monthan AFB aircraft display on July 19, 1990. This Phantom was returned to AMARG on February 19, 2014. (Nicholas A Veronico)

Opposite: It is fitting that F-4S BuNo. 157245, foreground, and F-4S 157249 are parked side-by-side, as these aircraft each downed a MiG-21 on May 6, 1972, while flying with the "Aardvarks" of VF-114 on board the USS *Kitty Hawk* (CVA-63). At the time, both Phantoms were F-4J models with 157245 flown by LCDR Kenneth W Pettigrew and LT (jg) Michael J McCabe, while 157249 was crewed by LT Robert G Hughes and LT (jg) Adolph J Cruz. Both air-to-air victories were achieved using AIM-9G Sidewinder missiles. BuNo. 157245 last flew with VMFA-251 and arrived at AMARG on August 29, 1985, while 157249's last squadron assignment was with VFMA-321, arriving at AMARG on October 30, 1986. The close-up shows the MiG-21 kill marking on 157249's air intake splitter plate. (Nicholas A Veronico)

The McDonnell Douglas F-15 first joined a USAF combat coded squadron in 1976, with its first aerial victory scored by an Israeli AF pilot in 1979. Since that time, pilots flying the Eagle have scored 104 aerial victories, with zero defeats being officially recognized. There is, however, a large price to pay for this success, with air combat training taking a toll in both terms of pilot lives and airframe losses and stress that, over time, can lead to retirement of the aircraft.

During Operation *Desert Storm*, 1st Lt David Sveden scored an aerial victory over an Iraqi Mirage F-1EQ fighter on January 19, 1991, while flying F-15C 79-0021. Sveden, a member of the 525th TFS, 36th Tactical Fighter Wing based at Incirlik AB, Turkey, downed the Mirage using an AIM-7 radar-homing missile. This "MiG killer" arrived at AMARG on June 18, 2010. (Both photos by Nicholas A Veronico)

On January 4, 1989, F-14A BuNo. 159437 (callsign Gypsy 202) and F-14A BuNo. 159610 (callsign Gypsy 207) each shot down a Libyan MiG-23 over the Mediterranean Sea, approximately 40 miles north of Tobruk. Based aboard the carrier USS *John F Kennedy*, the Tomcats from VF-32 were flying combat air patrol between the coast of Libya and the *Kennedy* when they were repeatedly engaged by a pair of Libyan MiG-23s. In spite of F-14s efforts to turn away multiple times and disengage from the MiGs, the Libyan pilots, guided by ground controllers, continued to pursue the Tomcats. Gypsy 207 fired two AIM-7 missiles that failed to find their target. The F-14s split horizontally when the MiGs returned head-on, and the Libyans began to pursue Gypsy 202, crewed by LT Herman C Cook III and LCDR Steven P Collins. The tail chase enabled Gypsy 207, crewed by CDR Joseph B Connelly and CDR Leo F Enwright, to fire again, downing the first of the MiGs. Gypsy 202 turned right and gained the advantage over the surviving MiG-23, which was brought down by an AIM-9 missile. Gypsy 207 has been preserved at the National Air and Space Museum's Steven F Udvar-Hazy Center in Chantilly, Virginia, while Gypsy 202 has been a resident of AMARG since February 11, 1992. (Nicholas A Veronico)

During Operation *Desert Storm*, Capt Donald Watrous of the 32nd Tactical Fighter Group was at the controls of F-15C 79-0022 when he encountered an Iraqi MiG-23 on January 28, 1991. As part of a flight of four Eagles patrolling along the Iraq–Iran border to prevent the Iraqi Air Force from escaping to Iran, Watrous was flying the number four jet. His wingman's radar was inoperable, so Watrous was given authority to engage. His first two AIM-7 missiles missed their target, so Watrous nosed his F-15 over while simultaneously dropping his three external fuel tanks, and when he did so, he heard a loud noise. Without the drag of the external tanks, Watrous went supersonic, closing the range to the MiG, and fired a third AIM-7. This also missed. Firing his last AIM-7, it impacted the MiG-23's starboard wing, and the Iraqi jet dove into the ground inverted. (Nicholas A Veronico)

Still showing its mark of aerial dominance, F-15C 79-0022 last served with the Oregon Air National Guard at Kingsley Field. (Jim Dunn)

On August 4, 2010, F-15C 79-0022 entered AMARG after 30 years of service. Six years later, the fighter had had a number of items removed, had been regenerated, and had returned to the Air Force F-15 Eagle fleet. It appeared that it would end its days at AMARG. (Nicholas A Veronico)

F-15C 79-0022 arrives at the Pueblo Weisbrod Aircraft Museum in Pueblo, Colorado, on board a lowboy hauler. Notice the radome tucked under the aircraft's fuselage near the starboard engine air intake. Upon arrival, museum officials set a hard deadline of four months to have the F-15 ready for display. (Pueblo Weisbrod Aircraft Museum via Shawn Kirscht)

F-15C 79-0022 as it looks today displayed at the Pueblo Weisbrod Aircraft Museum in Pueblo, Colorado. It is estimated that the restoration cost nearly $50,000 and involved nearly 8,000 labor hours to put the fighter into display condition. The beautifully restored Eagle has been the backdrop for a number of squadron reunions. (Pueblo Weisbrod Aircraft Museum via Shawn Kirscht)

On the third day of the Gulf War air campaign (January 19, 1991), Capt David Prather, flying F-15C 79-0069 from the 525th TFS, downed an Iraqi Mirage F-1. As the Iraqi Air Force attempted to flee to neighboring Iran, coalition armed forces lead by the United States formed a barrier to prevent aircraft from escaping. It was during these patrols, on January 19, that six Iraqi Air Force aircraft – two MiG-25s, two MiG-29s and a Mirage F-1 – were downed by F-15s. F-15C 79-0069 was delivered to AMARG for storage on August 10, 2010. The Eagle could be seen on the facility's Celebrity Row in June 2018, and departed AMARG on October 16, 2019, en route to Tyndall AFB, Florida. (Nicholas A Veronico)

MiG Killers in Storage			
Model	Serial	Victory Type	Date
F-4C	64-0699	MiG-17	April 23, 1966
F-4S	157245	MiG-21	May 6, 1972
F-4S	157249	MiG-21	May 6, 1972
F-14A	159437	MiG-23	January 4, 1989
F-15C	79-0021	Mirage F-1	January 19, 1991

Chapter 3

Bombers and Patrol Aircraft

Developed for the anti-submarine warfare (ASW) mission, the Lockheed S-3 Viking would serve the US Navy in that and several other roles from 1974 to 2016. Its final service would be with the "Bloodhounds" of VX-30 at NAS Point Mugu to patrol and maintain the safety of the offshore test ranges. On January 8, 2016, S-3B 160147/700 of VX-30 would be the last Viking to enter retirement at AMARG. Even though no other foreign service or civilian uses have been established for the Viking, there are now 108 of the 179 production aircraft still in storage at AMARG. (Jim Dunn)

Above and left: While the Commander Air Group's (CAG) aircraft will be the most colorful in each squadron, and will wear the modex ending in 00, individual squadron commanders' aircraft will often be given some color along with the 01 modex designation. (Modex is the two or three digit number worn on the nose of Navy and Marine Corps aircraft. This number is indicated by a slash when following the Bureau number.) The "World Famous and Internationally Traveled Screwbirds" of VS-33 operated the S-3 from 1975 until 2006, with S-3B 160121/701, being the final Viking, serving as the squadron commander's aircraft. It entered AMARG on June 27, 2006, after its last deployment aboard the USS *Carl Vinson*. (Jim Dunn)

Proudly wearing the look of a combat veteran, to go along with its name of "Bonesaw," S-3B 159390/700 entered AMARG on January 3, 2005, as the final CAG aircraft of the "Diamondcutters" of VS-30. Flying from the USS *Saratoga* during the Gulf War's Operation *Desert Storm*, several Vikings including 159390, then with the modex of 710, were given long-range surface surveillance duties as well as air-to-surface missions dropping Rockeye cluster bombs. (Jim Dunn)

Using the Big Safari program that allowed sole-source contracts, the USAF had General Dynamics modify 12 Martin B-57Bs and convert 9 RB-57Ds to create the RB-57F for high-altitude reconnaissance and air sampling. Now, with a wingspan of 122ft and powered by two TF33-P-11 turbofans in the wings and two underwing J60-P-9 turbojets, the aircraft could operate at a height of more than 60,000ft. They were assigned to the Air Weather Service headquartered at McClellan AFB, California, and operated in the China, India, and Pakistan theater when these countries were developing their nuclear programs. The 21 aircraft were given new serial numbers and eventually became WB-57Fs to denote a less clandestine weather mission. AMARG continues to support the three WB-57Fs that are still operational with NASA, with WB-57F 63-13302, which was retired on June 5, 1974, still available for harvesting parts. (Jim Dunn)

Above and right: After a long service in its intended ASW mission with the "Blue Dragons" of VP-50, and the "Pelicans" of VP-45, P-3C 158214/214 ended its career at NAS Jacksonville with the "Pros" of VP-30. Also known as the "Pros Nest," VP-30 is the Fleet Replenishment Squadron (FRS), training both US Navy and foreign crews on the Orion. While it was with VP-30, it retained the attractive gloss gray scheme that it had received when assigned to the "Pelicans" of VP-45. It entered the AMARG inventory on November 21, 2014. (Jim Dunn)

While many of the P-3C Orion fleet now in storage may soon face being scrapped, there are still a number of others just coming out of the fleet, as the Boeing P-8A Poseidon takes over their mission. New to AMARG on February 7, 2019, P-3C 158210/210 came from the "Totems" of VP-69, a Navy Reserve squadron based at NAS Whidbey Island, Washington. (Jim Dunn)

The "Bloodhounds" of VX-30 required several different types of aircraft in order to patrol the vast 42,000 square miles of sea and airspace that make up the Pacific Missile Test Range. Equipped with the billboard phased array telemetry antenna and the Extended Area Test System radar the NP-3D could conduct missions of up to 12 hours in length. Originally built as a P-3A, NP-3D 150522/340 was retired to AMARG on July 16, 2015. (Jim Dunn)

To go along with its Lockheed CP-140 Aurora version of the P-3C, the Canadian government also obtained three CP-140A Arcturus models. These examples did not have the anti-submarine capability, or anti-ship warfare mounts, of the Aurora. Based at CFB Greenwood, Nova Scotia, the principal mission would be crew training, as well as pollution, fishing, and smuggling patrol off the Canadian coast. Two of the aircraft – 140120 and 140121 – are still in residence at AMARG, having arrived in early 2011. (Nicholas A Veronico)

The last major upgrade to increase the performance of the Northrop Grumman E-2C Hawkeye was the NP2000 program. Beginning in 2004, Hawkeyes were given the Hamilton Sundstrand eight-blade, scimitar-shaped, carbon-fiber propellers that featured a steel leading edge. Each of the blades could be removed individually for ease of maintenance, and their installation reduced the vibration produced by the old four-blade propellers. Assigned to the "Greyhawks" of VAW-120, the FRS for the training of Hawkeye aircrew at NAS Norfolk, Virginia, TE-2C 164110/660 was used for pilot training prior to being retired on October 27, 2011. (Nicholas A Veronico)

Established in 1995 as the Navy's only fully dedicated counter-narcotics squadron, the "Nightwolves" of VAW-77 was a Navy Reserve unit operating four Grumman E-2C Hawkeyes out of NAS Atlanta, Georgia. The squadron would frequently make 60-day deployments throughout the Caribbean conducting anti-drug missions, with E-2C 161783/00 operating as its CAG aircraft until its retirement on March 10, 2005. (Nicholas A Veronico)

While assigned to the 405th TFW at Clark AB, Philippines, commanded by the then-Col Chuck Yeager, Martin B-57B 52-1545 was based with the 8th Bomb Squadron flying combat missions from Da Nang AB and Tan Son Nhut AB, in South Vietnam. In 1968, it would be sent to the MASDC at Davis-Monthan AFB before being converted to an EB-57B and assigned to the 134th Defense Systems Evaluation Squadron with the Vermont ANG. It would be sent back to MASDC for retirement on December 2, 1981. (Jim Dunn)

Above, left and below: The iconic overhead image of B-52s lying broken in the desert is a result of America complying with terms of the START. In order to count the B-52Gs as deployed strategic delivery vehicles under START, USAF teams cut up the 39 aircraft between October 2011 and December 2013. Each cut section was placed on a cradle 30 degrees off center and at least 6ft apart, enabling it to be viewed and counted by Russian satellites. (AMARG and Nicholas A Veronico)

B-52H 61-0023 was the first H model to be placed into storage, arriving on July 24, 2008, from the 20th Bomb Squadron, 2nd Bomb Wing at Barksdale AFB, Louisiana. The bomber is seen during a period of represervation, with the Spraylat removed from the cockpit and forward fuselage. Note the fading of the paint on the fuselage compared to the nose section showing the deeper gray color. The nose art, *Dimico Delectus*, translates as "I choose to lead the fight." This aircraft lost its tail during a low-level penetration training mission on January 10, 1964, when it encountered turbulence flying at 1,000ft above ground level. The crew, all Boeing employees on the test flight, were able to safely land the bomber at Blytheville AFB, Arkansas. Subsequently, all B-52s had their tails strengthened. This B-52 was repaired and it served for an additional 44 years. (Nicholas A Veronico)

The ability of the B-52H to operate fully loaded with the complete range of conventional aerial munitions has made it the most frequently called upon heavy bomber in the USAF. While the B-1B will soon disappear from the inventory, and the B-2 will be replaced by the B-21, the B-52H will continue to receive upgrades including new engines for those remaining in the fleet. With those like B-52H 61-0027, last assigned to the "Barons" of the 23rd BS at Minot AFB, North Dakota, continuing to be an important parts source for the future, some B-52Hs will no doubt make it past 75 years of service. (Jim Dunn)

Buffs over Orions: B-52s from Barksdale AFB, Louisiana, and Minot AFB, South Dakota, frame P-3s, C-9s, and C-130s against the Rincon Mountains, east of Tucson. This view provides a hint as to the size of AMARG and the volume of parts stored "on the wing," as only about 50 aircraft are visible out of the more than 3,100 in its inventory. The smallest aircraft type in storage is the TH-57 Sea Ranger helicopter, while the largest is the C-5A Galaxy airlifter. (Nicholas A Veronico)

When a Rockwell B-1B was sent to AMARG, it was often undetermined how long it would be in desert storage. In order to protect the sensitive electronic components on board, a custom-made bag was used to cover the forward section of fuselage in what was termed inviolate storage. Unfortunately for B-1B 86-0096, from the 37th BS at Ellsworth AFB, South Dakota, its fate has been to remain parked in the desert since arriving on September 17, 2002. (Nicholas A Veronico)

Above and below: Despite its operational issues, in Afghanistan and Iraq the B-1B Lancer has proven to be a very effective delivery platform for a wide range of conventional warheads. This scoreboard on the right nose gear door of B-1B 85-0065 displays its impressive bomb mission tally while assigned to the 28th BS at Dyess AFB, Texas. The "W" marked inside several of the bombs stands for "Winchester," which means that the full payload carried on that mission was dropped. Since September 26, 2012, 85-0065 has been providing critical components to keep other B-1Bs flying. (Jim Dunn)

B-1B 86-0096 served its entire career with the 37th Bomb Squadron, 28th Bomb Wing at Ellsworth AFB, South Dakota. The original "wolfpack" artwork showed a pack of four wolves and a full moon, but it was rather muted. New artwork by Steve Barba gave the Lancer some serious fangs and a menacing look. B-1B 86-0096 was the ninth of 15 B-1Bs that were retired between August 2002 and March 2003. (Nicholas A Veronico)

Chapter 4

Helicopters, Tankers, Trainers, and Transports

The Bell Model 206 JetRanger/LongRanger series are probably the most recognized helicopters in the world. Known as the OH-58 Kiowa or Kiowa Warrior, they served the US Army from 1969 to 2017. The first helicopter in this row is OH-58D 95-00010 that was retired from the 7th Squadron, 17th Cavalry Regiment at Fort Campbell, Kentucky on April 15, 2015. However, foreign military sales would see much of this row going to Greece, with 95-00010 departing on March 12, 2019. (Rick Turner)

Boeing Vertol CH-46F 156444 was accepted by the USMC on April 30, 1969, and assigned to the "Ridge Runners" of HMM-163. Converted to a CH-46E in September 1982, it would then serve with the "Moonlighters" of HMM-764, a Marine Reserve squadron that would be called to active duty for the Gulf War. Another deployment would come in 2005 when the squadron was sent to Al Asad, Iraq, to support Operation *Iraqi Freedom*. Lastly assigned to the "Wild Goose" of HMM-774, 156444/424 would retire to AMARG on April 10, 2015, nearly 46 years after being accepted. (Jim Dunn)

Accepted on February 12, 1970, as CH-46F 157682 this Sea Knight would be assigned to the "Nighthawks" of HMX-1 where it would serve for the next 44 years. Providing "Marine One" for the helicopter transport of the President, as well as support for other VIP travel, HMX-1 has operated a variety of rotor and tiltrotor aircraft for the mission. Included among those were a total of six Sea Knights that had been upgraded to CH-46E standards. Utilized to support presidential missions worldwide, CH-46E 157682/20 was finally retired to AMARG on March 11, 2014. (Nicholas A Veronico)

Home based at NAF Atsugi, Japan, with the "Warlords" of HSL-51, SH-60F 164081/01 was assigned to their Detachment 11 aboard the USS *Blue Ridge* (LCC-19) to support the Commander Seventh Fleet. As part of CVW-5 assigned to the USS *Ronald Reagan* HSL-51 was heavily involved in rescue and relief work after the enormous March 11, 2011, earthquake struck Japan. On December 11, 2013, SH-60F 164081/01 was retired to AMARG. However, its career was not ended, as it departed in November 2017 for new service with Israel. (Nicholas A Veronico)

The CAG-Bird for the "Dusty Dogs" of HS-7 sits poised on Mat 7 at NAS Fallon, Nevada, on July 28, 2009, during a two-year period that included workups and mini deployments such as earthquake relief in Haiti. From May to December 2010 SH-60F 164610/610 would embark for its final sea deployment with CVW-3 aboard the USS *Harry S Truman*. The squadron's Bulldog mascot now stands guard in Area 02 after being retired on February 24, 2011. (In service: Jim Dunn; In storage: Nicholas A Veronico)

Above and left: Many of the Sikorsky SH-60F Oceanhawks stored in Area 02 are now retained by the USCG to support its HH-60 Jayhawk fleet. This includes SH-60F 164087/10, the CAG-Bird for the "Warhawks" of HS-10, which was given this colorful paint scheme to mark the 50th anniversary of the squadron. It is seen here in February 2011 at NAS North Island during the celebration of 100 years of US Naval Aviation. (Jim Dunn)

Carrier Air Wing Five (CVW-5) has long been known for having some of the most colorful CAG aircraft in the US Navy. Based in Japan, these CAG-birds often feature scenes reflecting the culture of that country. Designed by LCDR Chrissy Dehner, the artwork on SH-60F 164460/610, from the "Chargers" of HS-14 at NAF Atsugi, Japan, highlights Mount Fuji and a massive rogue wave along its fuselage. Sadly, since entering AMARG on April 23, 2013, this beautiful artwork is fading into history. (Jim Dunn)

From its introduction in Vietnam in the early 1970s, to its workhorse roles during *Desert Storm* and other missions during the 1990s, to multiple deployments supporting the War on Terror, the CH-53 Sea Stallion has transported Marines into battle throughout the world. A total of 126 CH-53D model Sea Stallions were built for the Marines, with 38 of them, including 156968/07, being stored at AMARG. Assigned to the "Red Lions" of HMH-363 at MCB Kaneohe, Hawaii, this CH-53D was replaced by the revolutionary MV-22 Osprey and retired on June 16, 2011. (Jim Dunn)

Entering USMC service in 2008 the Bell UH-1Y Venom may well be the final new-build military variant of the famous Huey. Also known as the "Yankee," this model features a four-blade composite rotor, upgraded engine and transmission, along with a flat panel digital cockpit. A veteran of VMLAT-303, the USMC training squadron at Camp Pendleton, California, UH-1Y 166756/506 was sent to AMARG on May 14, 2018. (Jim Dunn)

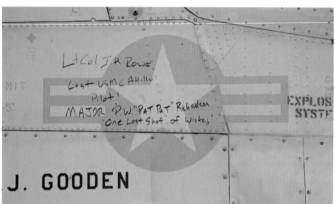

Above and left: After arriving on October 22, 2020, and first being processed through the flush farm, AH-1W 165051 is seen on December 3, 2020, on the South Maintenance Shelter ramp being prepared for desert storage in Area 15. Assigned to the "Nomads" of HMLA-773 Detachment A at JRB New Orleans, AH-1W 165051/20 was given the honor of closing out the 34-year history, and the more than 933,000 flight hours, of the AH-1W in USMC service. The crew of Lt Col J H Rowe and Maj P W "Pat" Richardson then signed off on "One Last Shot of Whiskey." (Jim Dunn)

Making its second visit to AMARG KC-130R 160626/626 was one of four Hercules ordered by the USAF but transferred to the USMC on completion. Assigned to the "Heavy Haulers" of VMGR-252 for both Operations *Desert Storm* and *Enduring Freedom*, it would then be relocated to Japan to serve with VMGR-152. When that squadron transitioned to the KC-130J, 160626 would make its first trip to AMARG before being brought back by the Navy to serve with Air Test and Evaluation Squadron VX-20 at NAS Patuxent River, Maryland. It would be retired to AMARG again on September 1, 2015. (Jim Dunn)

Above and right: Until being replaced by the MC-130J Commando II, the MC-130P Combat Shadow was the primary support aircraft for Air Force Special Operations Command (AFSOC). While providing infiltration, exfiltration, resupply, and limited command and control capabilities for special forces, its specialty was night low-level refueling support to AFSOC helicopters and tilt-wing aircraft. After making the final operational Combat Shadow flight for the 67th SOS at RAF Mildenhall on January 24, 2014, MC-130P 66-0215 would conclude its long service career with the 9th SOS at Eglin AFB, Florida, in November 2014, the same squadron that it deployed with during Operation *Desert Storm*. (Jim Dunn)

Seen in this row of Antarctic Operation *Deep Freeze* LC-130F/R Hercules aircraft is USCG HC-130H 1700, also a veteran of far-ranging service. Built as s/n 82-0081 it was the first in the series of HC-130H-7-LM Hercules delivered to USCG Air Station Clearwater, Florida, in May 1983. Over the next 32 years it would be stationed at Elizabeth City, New Jersey; Kodiak, Alaska; Sacramento, California, from which it is seen departing for a mission on January 21, 1989; and its final posting at Barbers Point, Hawaii. It was replaced in USCG service by the HC-130J and sent to AMARG on October 1, 2015. (Jim Dunn)

Boeing's KC-135 series of aerial refueling aircraft entered service in 1957 as the KC-135A. In the 1980s, the Air Force acquired a large number of retired commercial 707 jetliners, using their TF-33-PW-102 turbofan engines to upgrade the A models to E configuration. Air Force Reserve and Air National Guard units were the recipients of the 157 upgraded aircraft. The new engines were 14 percent more efficient, enabling the E model to offload 20 percent more fuel at greater range. The TF-33 engine conversion also brought thrust-reversing capabilities. The KC-135Es were parked between 2007 and 2009, as the type was replaced by the KC-135R fitted with CFM International F-108/CFM56 high-bypass turbofan engines.

Leading the line of KC-135Es is 59-1496 *Keystone Renegade* from the 171st Air Refueling Wing (ARW), Pennsylvania ANG, that arrived for storage on May 23, 2007. Landing at AMARG just seven days after *Keystone Renegade* is 56-3609 *For God and Country* from the 151st ARW, Tennessee ANG, with 57-1423 *Allegheny Warrior* from the 147th ARW, Pennsylvania ANG, third in line, having arrived on June 6, 2007. (Nicholas A Veronico)

Heritage is important to the USAF and it strives to maintain direct links to its past. One of the most famous B-17 units of World War Two was the "Bloody" 100th Bombardment Group (Heavy) based at RAF Thorpe Abbotts, and today its lineage is carried on by the 100th ARW now located at RAF Mildenhall. The 100th ARW has adorned its KC-135Rs with nose art and a "Square D" tail code to honor the courage and sacrifices made by its predecessors in the 100th BG. These reminders of the past can still be seen on KC-135R 61-0304, which ended its long service to the USAF on November 20, 2013. (Nicholas A Veronico)

In the history of the ANG, the most unusual and challenging transition from one type of aircraft to another took place in 1985 at Stewart ANGB, New York. At that time, the 137th Tactical Air Support Squadron had been flying the twin-engine, 2,848lb Cessna O-2A Super Skymaster since 1971 when it was tasked with becoming the first ANG squadron to operate the 321,000lb C-5A Galaxy. With nose art honoring the B-17G *Aluminum Overcast*, one of the few Flying Fortresses still being flown today, C-5A 70-0464 would fly into retirement at AMARG on September 17, 2012, after the 137th AS converted to the C-17A. (Jim Dunn)

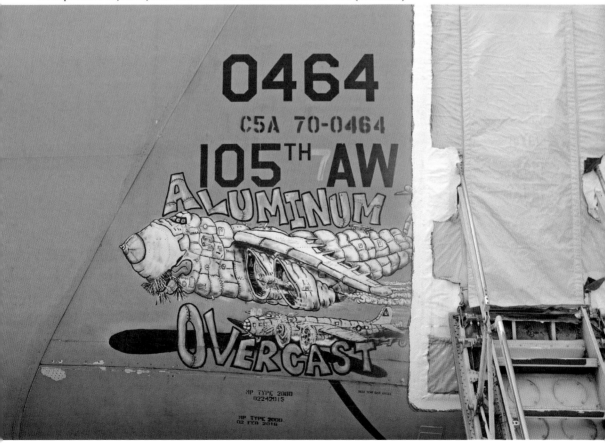

For most of the first generation of Lockheed C-5A Galaxy airlifters, their service career would end with a tour of duty on a Reserve or ANG squadron. The tail bands on this line-up of C-5As represents squadrons that had both a long and rather brief history operating the Galaxy. The 167th AW of the West Virginia ANG at Martinsburg would transition to the C-5A in 2006 after having flown the Lockheed C-130 Hercules for 34 years. Its association with the Galaxy would only last until 2014 when it would then transition to the Boeing C-17 Globemaster III. It was a different story for the "Alamo Wing" 433rd AW at Kelly AFB, Texas, which in 1985 would become the first Reserve organization to receive the C-5. Today the wing is flying the C-5M, the latest model in this famous line. (Jim Dunn)

Lockheed C-5A Galaxy 69-0025 entered AMARG on April 8, 2015, after its final service with the 167th AW of the West Virginia ANG. What attracts attention, however, is the famous nose art that was applied by its previous unit, the 164th AW of the Tennessee ANG at Memphis ANGB. The legend of the B-17F that first carried the name *Memphis Belle* is one of the best-known histories of World War Two, and the USAF has allowed the name and artwork to be passed on to later aircraft. The list of these aircraft includes an A-10A, B-52G, B-52H, F-15E, F-105D, FB-111A, and the latest C-17A named *Memphis Belle XI*. Though C-5A 69-0025 *Memphis Belle X* does not carry the artwork on both sides, if it did, the bathing suit would be painted red on the right side. (Jim Dunn)

The Beechcraft T-34C Mentor would begin service with the Navy in 1975 as its primary training aircraft. Now replaced in this role by the Beechcraft T-6B Texan II, the T-34C continues to serve in small roles such as a range safety aircraft. The Mentors in this row are from Training Air Wing Five (TAW-5) at Whiting Field, Florida, which is home to three primary fixed-wing and three advanced helicopter squadrons. In the foreground T-34C 161032/032 was retired on June 26, 2012. (Nicholas A Veronico)

Above and right: Civilian contractors have played a major role in the Navy service history of the North American T-39 Sabreliner. Used to train Naval Flight Officers in both navigation and radar intercepts, the T-39s were mostly flown and maintained by civilians. A total of 17 former civilian Sabreliners were obtained and designated T-39N in order to meet advances in radar technology. These aircraft were also given civilian registrations, T-39N 165516 was N308NT when it was operated with the "Sabrehawks" of VT-86 and the "Rubber Ducks" of VT-4. It was retired to AMARG on August 28, 2014. (Jim Dunn)

1963-2014

51
Years
T-39 SABRELINER

CDR Samuel White
VT-4 CO

Pieter VandenBergh
Chief Pilot

Russ Early

Mike Neri
T-39 Site Manager

Chuck Kneemiller
T-39 Maint Manager

Serving for 37 years, first at Mather AFB, California, and then at Randolph AFB, Texas, the Boeing T-43A was the navigator training aircraft for the USAF. Based on the 737-253, there would be 19 built, with final retirement from this role coming in December 2010. Four of the six T-43As remaining at AMARG can be seen here, with 71-1404 arriving on January 26, 2010, from the 562nd FTS at Randolph AFB. (Nicholas A Veronico)

Assigned to the United States Army Priority Transport Command (USAPAT) and stationed at JB Pearl Harbor–Hickam, Hawaii, C-20F 91-0108 *Victory* traveled the world for 25 years supporting US Army missions. This command/executive staff transport was modified from a Gulfstream G-IV to carry up to 14 passengers and a crew of five. *Victory* would be flown to AMARG on July 25, 2018, to join seven other Gulfstream executive transports already in storage there. (Jim Dunn)

Many of the Douglas/McDonnell Douglas TA-4J Skyhawk trainers have, or will soon have, passed the 30-years-in-storage mark. These light attack aircraft served with both the US Navy and Marine Corps, with the Marines phasing the type out in 1998 and the Navy in 2003. The TA-4J is a dedicated trainer, not equipped with a weapons system, and fitted with a down-rated 8,500lb thrust Pratt & Whitney J52-P-6B turbojet engine. A total of 281 TA-4Js were built and more than 50 TA-4Fs were converted to this configuration. The first four TA-4Js in this long line are (from left to right): TA-4Js BuNo. 156909, which last flew with Training Wing Two (TW-2), which was parked at AMARG on October 23, 1991; 153495 from the "Fighting Saints" of Fighter Squadron Composite One-Three (VFC-13), which arrived on July 7, 1993; 158095 from TW-2 joining others on July 28, 1992; and 158117, also from TW-2, which arrived on August 18, 1994. With A-4s out of service with all but a few air arms, the type will soon meet the scrapper's torch. (Nicholas A Veronico)

With Greece being the only other country that is still operating small numbers of the North American T-2 Buckeye, the Defense Logistics Agency has determined it is no longer necessary to maintain a large inventory at AMARG to support the mission. Soon this row of Buckeyes, which introduced thousands of naval aviators to carrier aviation from 1959 to 2004, will join a number of others being turned over to the scrapper for final processing. (Jim Dunn)

Chapter 5

Special Use Aircraft

Deployed throughout the world in support of operations such as *Enduring Freedom* and *Iraqi Freedom*, Beechcraft RC-12N 88-00327 Guardrail was assigned to Bravo Company of the 224th Military Intelligence Battalion at Hunter Army Airfield, Fort Stewart, Georgia. Based on the Beechcraft King Air, the RC-12N was a signal intelligence (SIGNIT) gathering platform conducting surveillance and reconnaissance flights in support of Army ground commanders. Replaced by more advanced manned and unmanned platforms, RC-12N 88-00327 was retired on April 13, 2015. (Jim Dunn)

Grumman EA-6B Prowler 163399 (Modex 500) would have an interesting and colorful Navy service history. In 1991, while assigned to the "Zappers" of VAQ-130 aboard the USS *John F Kennedy*, it would be credited with firing eight AGM-88 High-Speed Anti-Radiation Missiles, known as HARMs, in what is reported to be their first operational use by a Prowler. Later it would become the CAG aircraft for two different squadrons, first with the very colorful flag markings of the "Patriots" of VAQ-140, and then with its final squadron the somewhat less colorful "Wizards" of VAQ-133. It is seen here with the "Patriots" during a *Red Flag* exercise at Nellis AFB on February 14, 2008, and at AMARG after its retirement on May 14, 2013. (Jim Dunn)

Above and right: One of the stars on what was formerly known as "Celebrity Row" at AMARG, a main road lined with examples of the types in storage, is Northrop Grumman E-8C 90-0175 Joint STARS. Standing for "Joint Surveillance Target Attack Radar System," JSTARS can track up to 600 ground targets within a 150-mile area, providing airborne command and control for battlefield managers. Only 16 E-8C JSTARS were produced, and the USAF has decided not to replace them with another manned aircraft. Arriving on January 21, 2015, E-8C 90-0175 can now be seen along what is now called "Display Row" at AMARG. (Jim Dunn)

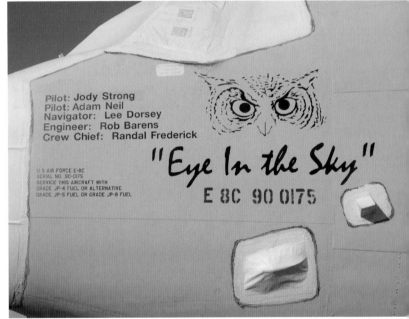

Rescued from a Florida boneyard in 1988, former Pan American *Clipper Seven Seas*, N404PA, would embark on a new career as a test platform operated jointly by the USAF 305th Electronic Systems Wing and Massachusetts Institute of Technology's Lincoln Laboratory. Now named *Sashambre* and based at Hanscom AFB, it would test antennas, image systems, radio frequency and laser communication technologies for supporting airborne battle management systems. Given the USAF serial number 18835, it was retired to AMARG on October 26, 2020, becoming a source of spares to support the remaining military aircraft based on the 707 airframe. (Nicholas A Veronico)

The US Army's Airborne Reconnaissance Low aircraft, designated EO-5C, are a manned, multi-sensor, all-weather intelligence, surveillance, and reconnaissance platform. Sensors on board can collect communications intelligence and imagery intelligence (COMINT/IMINT) using its ground moving target indicator/synthetic aperture radar and electro-optical and infrared full-motion video capabilities. This information provides real-time situational awareness to battlefield commanders on the ground.

Sensor technology changes and engine efficiency improvements have led to the replacement of the type. Beginning in FY 21, the EO-5C is being replaced by the Airborne Reconnaissance Low-Enhanced aircraft, designated EO-6C, based on a modified, twin-engine, de Havilland Canada DHC-8-Q315 equipped with a reconfigurable COMINT/IMINT sensor load capability.

In December 2020, four of the type had been parked at AMARG. The first to arrive for storage was EO-5C 99-0056 (N566CC) on August 29, 2016, with EO-5C (99-0076) N176RA on August 8, 2017. On May 23, 2019, 99-0065 (N765MG) arrived and was followed by EO-5C (99-0104) N53993 on January 23, 2020. N765MG is parked on the facility's Display Row. (Nicholas A Veronico)

Located on Display Row, NASA DC-9-30, N932NA, is seen shortly after its arrival on February 25, 2016. Delivered to KLM Royal Dutch Airlines in February 1970, as PH-DNZ *City of Rome*, it then served a short time with the Venezuelan airline VIASA as YV-139C before going to the US Navy as C-9B 162754 in June 1983. NASA flew it as a "Zero-G" trainer in January 2004. AMARG has been the final stop for many NASA aircraft over several decades. (Jim Dunn)

Some aircraft at AMARG have contributed just about all there is to give to help maintain others of their type in service. For EP-3E 148887, there is little left after 26 years in the desert. The first of ten early model P-3As to be converted to an ARIES (Airborne Reconnaissance Integrated Electronic Systems) platform, this veteran of Operations *Desert Shield* and *Desert Storm* with the "World Watchers" of VQ-1, based at NAS Agana, Guam, may soon find the scrapper calling. (Jim Dunn)

Lockheed P-3C-II was delivered to VX-1 on October 10, 1977. For its first 30 years of service, 160291 flew with VX-1, VP-30, and VP-11, with assignments to the Naval Air Development Center and the Naval Air Warfare Center – Aircraft Division, before it was modified at Waco, Texas to EP-3E configuration. After modification, 160291 spent the rest of its career with VQ-1 based at NAS Whidbey Island, Washington. It arrived at AMARG on December 16, 2014. (Nicholas A Veronico)

In the early 1990s, 16 Lockheed S-3A Vikings were modified with the Tactical Airborne Signals Exploitation System to replace aging EA-3B Skywarriors. Designated ES-3A, with the nickname "Queer Viking," these aircraft provided electronic reconnaissance, searching out indications and warnings of threats to the carrier battle group. Assigned to the "Sea Shadows" of VQ-5 at NAS Agana, Guam, and then NAS North Island, California, ES-3A 159405/725 was retired to AMARG on June 7, 1999, when all of the Queer Vikings were stood down. (Jim Dunn)

Unusual aircraft have always been a part of the mystique of AMARG. Some may be exotic military types such as the Lockheed D-21 drone, or common civilian aircraft like the Boeing 737s known as "JANET" that provided daily transport to Area 51 and other clandestine locations. An ex-JANET aircraft, Boeing 737-247, serial number 19605, began life as a commercial airliner for Western Airlines. It made its first flight on August 12, 1968, and was delivered to the carrier on August 20 of that year. Acquired by EG&G in December 1980 for use as a JANET transport, ownership passed to Westinghouse in September 1995. Northrop Grumman acquired the jetliner for use as a test bed, registered it N165W, and fitted it with various protuberances including this large camera port and an infrared turret under the nose. Arriving at AMARG on November 4, 2011, the jet was carried on the inventory as a T-43A. After all its useful parts were reclaimed, the ex-Western Airlines 737 was scrapped on November 4, 2011. (Jim Dunn, close-up Nicholas A Veronico)

US Navy TC-18F BuNo. 165342 was originally built by Boeing as a 707-382B commercial jetliner, serial number 18961, for the Portuguese airline TAP. The jetliner was delivered on December 16, 1965, named *Santa Cruz*, and registered CS-TBA. In May 1985, CS-TBA was acquired by Air Atlantis. Two years later, the Boeing jetliner was sold to Atlantic Leasing and Financial, which registered the aeroplane N45RT in February 1987. It, in turn, leased the aircraft to Reflectone Training Systems. Buffalo Holdings, Inc. acquired the jetliner on November 26, 1991. After two years of service, the aircraft was acquired by the US Navy and designated a TC-18F. Based at Tinker AFB, Oklahoma, it was flown by Fleet Air Reconnaissance Squadron Seven (VQ-7) for E-6A Mercury crew proficiency training. As seen in this December 2020 view, the aircraft has yielded quite a number of parts to keep others of its type flying. (Nicholas A Veronico)

Delivered to United Airlines from the Douglas Aircraft Company factory in Long Beach, California, on September 28, 1966, this DC-8-54F freighter, serial number 45881, was registered N8048U. After hauling freight for United Airlines, the aircraft was acquired by Electrospace Systems of Richardson, Texas, on November 13, 1984. Converted for the Navy, it was designated EC-24A, taken on strength on June 15, 1987, and assigned BuNo. 163050.

This was the only EC-24A operated by the Navy and was used as an electronic warfare aggressor aircraft. Radomes cover electronic countermeasures jamming antennas, receivers used for enemy radar/signal identification, and secure communications systems antennas. In addition, the aircraft could fill the air with radar obscuring chaff capable of covering the A to J radar bands. A typical mission crew included pilot, co-pilot, flight engineer, mission commander, and six systems operators. The EC-24A arrived for storage on December 10, 1998, and today resides on Display Row. (Ron Strong)

Above and left: In the late 1970s, the North Atlantic Treaty Organization (NATO) decided to form its own Airborne Early Warning and Control Force, which led to the purchase of 18 Boeing E-3A Sentry AWACS aircraft. Registered to the then non-existent Luxembourg Air Force and assigned to a NATO base at Geilenkirchen, West Germany, these AWACS aircraft conducted patrols worldwide using multinational crews. After 32 years and 22,206 hours of service, it was decided that E-3A LXN90449 (79-0449) would be retired to AMARG on June 24, 2015, to become a source of spare parts valued at up to $40 million. Since then, two other NATO E-3A AWACS have been sent for storage including LXN90458, which arrived on September 12, 2018. This aircraft from Number 1 Squadron wears the markings and the motto "Hard To Be Humble" from the June 2017 Tiger Meet held at Naval Air Base Landivisiau, France. At the bottom is Boeing C-137B 68-19997, NATO serial number LXN19997. This aircraft is officially a CT-49A used for AWACS crew training. (Jim Dunn and Nicholas A Veronico)

Chapter 6

Centennial of Naval Aviation Paint Schemes

Naval aviation training began in 1911, when the Navy took advantage of Glenn H Curtiss' offer to train one officer how to fly a flying boat – free of charge. Then-LT Theodore G "Spuds" Ellyson was selected and his training began at a location in San Diego Bay, California, that is today NAS North Island. That same year, after Ellyson completed his training, the Navy purchased a Curtiss A-1 Triad as its first aircraft.

In honor of the US Navy's 100th anniversary, the service undertook a heritage paint project to highlight its history. The project's goal was to create public awareness of the Navy's 100 years of service protecting the United States and its interests around the globe as well as improving the USCG, Marine Corps, and Navy's internal appreciation of its own heritage. The effort, known as the Centennial of Naval Aviation (CONA), selected aircraft that were emerging from overhaul that would need new paint and those that were not slated to be deployed overseas. This minimized the costs involved and maximized the public relations value of aircraft participating in the centennial celebrations.

Every program must have an inspiring logo and the CONA is no exception. The project's logo features a Curtiss-built A-1 Triad biplane, circa 1911, and one of today's Lockheed Martin F-35B Lightning IIs in flight over the naval aviator's wings of gold. The logo was designed by then-LT Ian Espich in collaboration with CAPT Richard Dann, executive director of the project.

The CONA staff selected a total of 29 aircraft to participate in the project – one airship, six helicopters, and 22 fixed-wing aircraft. Eighteen of the aircraft came from the fleet and 11 from Training Command, with the first aircraft completed in July 2010 and the final finished in summer 2013. These aircraft, all wearing retro paint schemes, were seen at airshows, on TV, and in newspapers and magazines across the country, representing the history of the Navy, Marine Corps, and USCG.

As each aircraft's time in the service came to a close, retirement plans were put in place. A couple of the CONA aircraft were given new homes in base heritage air parks where they can be appreciated by service members and the public alike. Ten of the special paint scheme CONA aircraft are, or were, stored at AMARG.

T-34C BuNo. 161841 wears the tail code "G" to represent its assignment with Training Air Wing Four (TAW-4), based at Corpus Christi, Texas. The turboprop-powered T-34C Mentor was used for primary and intermediate pilot training. The CONA color scheme on 161841 represents a Vought SB2U Vindicator assigned to the USS *Ranger* (CV-4) Air Group in 1938. This T-34C flew into AMARG for storage on August 14, 2013. (Jim Dunn)

Training Air Wing Five (TAW-5) based at NAS Whiting Field, Florida, conducts 60 percent of all Navy and Marine Corps flight training activities. T-34C BuNo. 164172 was assigned to TAW-5, tail code "E," when it gained this heritage paint scheme representing the standard colors of a pre-World War Two Marine Corps aircraft.

The Hawker Beechcraft T-34C turbo Mentor served the US Navy and Marine Corps for more than 35 years with the type replaced by the T-6 Texan II turboprop trainer, also built by Hawker Beechcraft. T-34C 164172 retired to AMARG on August 14, 2013. Four years later, in October 2017, the National Museum of the Marine Corps loaned this aircraft to the Pima Air and Space Museum, adjacent to AMARG, to give the public the opportunity to see the T-34C Mentor in its retro paint scheme. (Nicholas A Veronico)

Training Squadron Three Five (VT-35), known as the "Stingrays," is one of the Navy's two advanced, multi-engine training squadrons. This is the last stop before naval aviators join the fleet flying the EP-3 Aries, MV-22 Osprey tiltrotor, or the P-8 Poseidon. Pilots at this advanced stage of training are gaining experience flying on instruments, in formation flying, as well as over-water navigation and low-level tactical maneuvers. TC-12B BuNo. 161197 was finished in an early World War Two heritage scheme to commemorate the aircraft flown at the Battle of the Coral Sea in May 1942. This aircraft arrived at AMARG on August 3, 2016. (Nicholas A Veronico)

North American Aviation T-39N BuNo. 165523 was flown by the Sabrehawks of Training Squadron Eight-Six (VT-86), a component of Training Air Wing Six (TAW-6) based at NAS Pensacola, Florida. This Sabreliner wears the colors of a pre-war, circa 1938, fighter from the USS Enterprise (CV-6) Air Group while maintaining the "F" tail code representing its modern-day group identification letter. BuNo. 165523 was retired to AMARG on May 22, 2014. (Nicholas A. Veronico)

S-3B Viking BuNo. 160581 wears an early World War Two tactical paint scheme, the same as those worn by fighters of the day. The Naval Air Test and Evaluation Squadron Three Zero (VX-30) Viking was undergoing maintenance and repair at Fleet Readiness Center Southeast (FRCSE), NAS Jacksonville, Florida, when it was selected to receive a CONA paint scheme. VX-30 commanding officer, CDR John Rousseau; CAPT Richard Dann, the CONA project's executive director and subsequent director of history and outreach; and FRCSE S-3 Viking planner, Don Lockwood, collaborated on the paint scheme that incorporates the VX-30 "Bloodhounds" logo on the tail. BuNo. 160581 arrived at AMARG on November 3, 2015, and today resides on Display Row. (Nicholas A Veronico)

Close-up of the CONA logo on P-3C BuNo. 161329. This Orion was delivered to VP-11 on May 5, 1981. Nine years later it moved to the West Coast P-3 training squadron VP-31 at NAS Moffett Field, California, followed by assignments to VP-40, VP-10, VP-94, VP-65, and VP-64 before undergoing the P-3C BMUP (Block Modification Upgrade Program, essentially bringing this aircraft up to P-3C III standards) in July 2003. The BMUP saw 25 aircraft converted to carry the ASQ-227 mission computer and ASQ-78B avionics suite. Following its modification, 161329 flew with VP-92, VP-62, VP-45, VP-8, and returned to VP-62 in May 2010. Here it wore the tail markings of Commander, Patrol and Reconnaissance Wing 11 (CPRW-11). P-3C 161329 arrived at AMARG on March 25, 2014. (Nicholas A Veronico)

The Consolidated PBY Catalina patrol bomber was instrumental at the Battle of Midway (June 4–7, 1942). PBYs discovered the Japanese invasion and the mobile force heading to attack Midway. They also sighted Japanese aircraft en route to attack and were able to warn American forces before the battle began. A VP-44 PBY-5A, call sign "Strawberry 5," was flown by LT Howard P Ady Jr and it was this aircraft's crew that sighted the Japanese aircraft carriers approaching the island.

P-3C BuNo. 161591 pays tribute to the bravery of Strawberry 5's crew with 1942-period camouflage as well as the aircraft's fuselage code "44-P-4" (squadron number, "P" for "patrol," and aircraft number). The aircraft's centennial paint scheme certainly stands out among the row of gray Orions. BuNo. 161591 arrived at AMARG for storage on September 14, 2014. Note the Royal Air Force Harriers at the end of the line. (Both Nicholas A Veronico)

P-3C BuNo. 158206 wears the late 1960s paint scheme of an EP-3B "Bat Rack" Orion. Two aircraft were modified to Bat Rack configuration to specifically monitor Soviet shipping during the Vietnam War. These Orions were later upgraded to EP-3E configuration. BuNo. 158206 was delivered on February 3, 1971, and flew with Air Test and Evaluation Squadron One (VX-1), Special Projects Patrol Squadron One (VPU-1), VP-26, VP-30 and received its CONA paint scheme in January 2011, while serving with Fleet Air Reconnaissance Squadron Two (VQ-2). It subsequently served with VQ-1 from August 2012 until it was flown to storage on October 1, 2013. (Nicholas A Veronico)

Chapter 7

"What Happened to _____?"

What Happened to the 747 Airborne Laser Airplane?

During the first Gulf War (August 1990–March 1991), Iraq launched a number of SS-1 "scud" ballistic missiles at neighboring Israel and Saudi Arabia. The scuds were fired from truck-mounted mobile launchers that would shoot the missiles and then pick up and drive to another location. To counter the launches, Air Force A-10 Thunderbolt II attack aircraft hunted for the scuds during the day, while F-15E Eagles attempted to locate launch operations at night using infrared targeting pods and surface search radar. The massive effort expended by the Air Force in hunting for the scud's mobile infrastructure demonstrated the need for a new method of combating theater-deployed ballistic missiles.

US military strategists envisioned a fleet of seven highly modified Boeing 747s fitted with high-energy lasers orbiting outside a hostile country's borders, patrolling for missile launches. During the boost phase of the missile's ascent, the laser-equipped 747 would detect and lock onto the target, determine the weather between the target and the missile, and adjust for any atmospheric conditions – such as rain or other atmospheric water vapor – and then fire the laser destroying a missile.

To prove the theory, in 2001 the DoD's Missile Defense Agency put the concept out to bid and awarded a procurement contract to a Boeing-led team with the 747-builder providing the aircraft, Northrop Grumman the laser, and Lockheed Martin developing the fire control system and the nose turret. The result was the YAL-1 Airborne Laser Test Bed, a Boeing 747-400 freighter (Air Force serial number 00-0001, manufacturer's serial number 30201/line number 1238) jam-packed with the infrastructure to initiate and fire a one-megawatt chemical oxygen iodine laser (referred to as a COIL laser).

The directed-energy equipped, airborne laser proof-of-concept 747 turned science fiction into science fact on the evening of February 2, 2010, when a solid-fuel rocket was destroyed and again on February 11, 2010, when a sea-launched, liquid-fueled ballistic missile was tracked and destroyed by the high-flying YAL-1. Both successful tests took place off the Southern California coast.

In subsequent months, the airborne laser test bed suffered some setbacks and achieved additional successes. But having proven the technology, the program became a target for budget cuts. Coupled with the Defense Department's vision of more powerful, yet smaller airborne lasers, funding for the 747 airborne laser was terminated in 2012. On February 14 of that year, the YAL-1 made its last flight, from its home at Edwards Air Force Base, California to the Air Force Materiel Command's 309th AMARG, located at Davis-Monthan Air Force Base, outside Tucson, Arizona. Here, the flying laser test bed was preserved and put into storage. During the course of its 15-year technology demonstration, the aircraft flew 206 missions, acquiring 250 cycles (each cycle is one take off and one landing) and 954 flight hours.

The end of the airborne laser test bed program did not mean the end of aircraft fitted with directed-energy weapons. In January 2013, the Defense Advanced Research Projects Agency (DARPA) began studying the development of 150kW lasers through its High-Energy Liquid Laser Area Defense System (HELLADS) program. DARPA envisions these weapons fitted to fighters and bombers, enabling them to shoot down enemy air-to-air or ground-launched missiles. HELLADS is just one of a number of directed-energy weapons programs under development today by various armed services and research agencies in the United States.

To Keep Others Flying

AMARG's job is to provide a stockpile of parts to America and her Allies' military aircraft fleets and store a variety of aircraft in various states of readiness, ranging from those capable of returning to flight within days or weeks to those undergoing the parts reclamation process that will eventually be scrapped once their carcasses are picked clean.

Having placed the YAL-1 into storage at AMARG's facility, a new operator was sought for the test bed. With no takers and no economical way to reconfigure the YAL-1, the Missile Defense Agency decided to let AMARG do what it does best: return parts to the fleet to keep others flying. As the YAL-1 sat in storage, the Missile Defense Agency offered both the Air Force and NASA the opportunity to acquire parts from the airborne laser test bed – the Air Force operating "Air Force One" and the E-4B airborne command post (both types are highly modified 747-200s), and NASA's flying telescope, the Stratospheric Observatory for Infrared Astronomy (SOFIA) is a 747SP (Special Performance).

In an excellent demonstration of planning and teamwork, the E-4B operators received the majority of the YAL-1's control surfaces and exterior panels while NASA sought actuators, motors, and other components inside the wing. This recycling effort saved the US taxpayer approximately $15 million and was of huge benefit to the government's 747 operators.

The YAL-1 was scrapped at the end of September 2014.

Having successfully completed its objectives, the YAL-1 Airborne Laser Test Bed aircraft was flown to storage at the Aircraft Maintenance and Regeneration Group's facility adjacent to Davis-Monthan Air Force Base, Tucson, Arizona. The aircraft arrived for storage on February 14, 2012. (Nicholas A Veronico)

Mission markings on the YAL-1 show nine operational sorties with two missile kills, one a solid-fuel rocket and the other a sea-launched, liquid-fueled ballistic missile. These targets were tracked and destroyed while the YAL-1 was most likely flying at 37,000ft and Mach 0.85. (Nicholas A Veronico)

Through careful planning, the Air Force's E-4 (military 747) operators were able to start the parts reclamation process first. Here, NASA technicians have arrived to remove parts that will be beneficial to their 747 program. (Nicholas A Veronico)

Empty flap tracks and oddly hanging landing gear doors greeted NASA mechanics when they came to remove parts from the Missile Defense Agency's YAL-1 airborne laser test bed. Air Force E-4 technicians previously removed a number of large components, such as flaps, giving NASA access to the YAL-1's interior pumps and piping. The transfer of parts from one agency to another was a tremendous cost savings to the US taxpayer. (Nicholas A Veronico)

Above: When the parts reclamation process was finished, the external appearance of the YAL-1 had not changed much. Gear doors, flaps, and other external parts were gone, but the majority of the parts returned to inventory were taken from internal flight systems. (Nicholas A Veronico)

Right: NASA technicians carefully remove parts from inside the YAL-1's starboard wing slats. Valves, actuators, and pumps are all components that were removed from the airborne laser test bed, inspected, overhauled, tagged, and added to NASA's 747 parts inventory. (Nicholas A Veronico)

What Happened to Blue Angels Number 7?

The US Navy Flight Demonstration Team, the Blue Angels, retired F/A-18B BuNo. 161711 to AMARG on June 29, 2010. The number seven jet is used for media orientation flights, flown as a backup aircraft in case one of the team's planes is grounded for a maintenance issue, and often provides an aerial survey of a show site before the team arrives.

Blue Angels F/A-18B BuNo. 161711 joined the team in October 2009. It had previously flown in the fleet as an adversary training aircraft with "The Fighting Saints" of Fighter Squadron Composition One-Three (VFC-13) at NAS Fallon, Nevada, before joining the Blue Angels.

While in storage at AMARG, 161711 spent a number of years on Display Row, where it was seen by close to 25,000 visitors annually. The bus tour from the Pima Air and Space Museum always makes a stop at Display Row, and the former Blue Angels F/A-18 attracted a lot of attention.

A request for an F/A-18 cockpit was made from NAS Pensacola, Florida, as one of the units there needed a procedures trainer. The forward fuselage of 161711 was selected to fill this request, and it was soon removed, crated, and shipped to NAS Pensacola. After regenerating all usable parts from the remainder of the aircraft, the hulk was sold to the commercial metal recycler HVF West LLC, Tucson, to be scrapped. What was left of BuNo. 161711 was transported out of AMARG on September 11, 2018.

Having flown the legacy F/A-18 Hornet for more than 35 years, the Blue Angels received its first F/A-18E Super Hornet on July 27, 2020, when it was delivered to the team's home base at NAS Pensacola, Florida. The Super Hornets joining the team all came from fleet squadrons and were modified for aerial demonstration use with the addition of an oil tank used to generate smoke, an inverted fuel system that enables team planes to fly for extended periods inverted, civilian air traffic

Above: Blue Angles F/A-18 BuNo. 161711 was displayed along AMARG's Celebrity Row for a number of years and is seen here on August 28, 2012. (Nicholas A Veronico)

Left: Four years later, BuNo. 161711 had lost its forward fuselage and cockpit, seen here on March 29, 2016. (Nicholas A Veronico)

control compatible navigation equipment, cameras and camera mounts, and adjustments to the stick "feel" as well as the aircraft's center of gravity.

During the remainder of 2020 and spring of 2021, the team will be transitioning to the Super Hornet. The first shows will take place in 2021, the team's 75th anniversary season.

What Happened to the XC-99 Giant Cargo Plane?

During World War Two, Consolidated Vultee Aircraft (later to become Convair) was tasked with building a bomber with intercontinental range. That aeroplane became the Convair B-36 Peacemaker, a massive aircraft with a fuselage length of 183ft and a wingspan of 230ft. The B-36 was powered by six 28-cylinder, 3,800hp Pratt & Whitney R-4360-53 Wasp Major engines and four General Electric J47 turbojet engines of 5,200lbf thrust each. This massive aircraft could carry 72,000lbs of bombs.

Army Air Force planners asked themselves, if a B-36 could carry 72,000lbs of bombs, what could a cargo version of the bomber carry? Stripping out all of the B-36's offensive and defensive armament would give a cargo version more capacity, and with that a single prototype was born. Assigned the designation XC-99 and serial number 43-52436, the prototype made its first flight on November 24, 1947. Gone were the jet engines, and the radials had been changed to 3,500hp R-4360-41 engines. In place of the bomb load and defensive gun turrets, room for 400 fully loaded troops or 335 litter patients, the capacity to carry 100,000lbs (45,000kg) of cargo became the hallmark of the XC-99.

The XC-99 flew with the US Air Force from July 1950 until March 19, 1957, hauling cargo across both the Atlantic and Pacific Oceans racking up more than 7,400 flight hours having transported more than 60 million pounds of cargo. Retired to Kelly AFB, Texas, the aircraft sat outside in the weather for 47 years until the decision was made to dismantle the XC-99 and transport it to the National Museum of the US Air Force in Dayton, Ohio, in 2004. The process took until 2008, when the entire aircraft was at the museum. Beginning in 2014, large sections of the XC-99, including the wings, engine nacelles, and aft fuselage were moved to AMARG for storage until the Air Force Museum can take on the restoration of this 1950s airlifter.

Convair's XC-99 in flight over Southern California in the early 1950s. Notice the six, pusher engines installed on the wing's trailing edge. Only one XC-99 was built. (National Museum of the US Air Force)

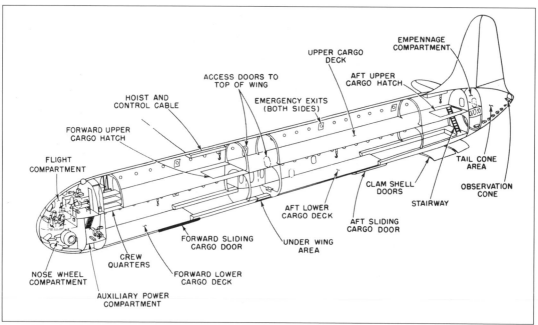

Cut-away diagram showing the various compartments of the XC-99. Cannon and small vehicles could be lifted into the fuselage and stored on the lower deck using the clamshell doors under the aft fuselage. (National Museum of the US Air Force)

Upper forward fuselage and cockpit window frames of the XC-99 in storage. The aircraft's massive size, coupled with a lack of storage space at the National Museum of the US Air Force in Dayton, Ohio, required that the giant cargo aeroplane be stored in the desert. In addition, climatic conditions at AMARC favor the long-term health of the aircraft. (Nicholas A Veronico)

Inside the lower aft fuselage looking to the rear of the aircraft showing the emergency exits on both sides, the starboard observer's chair, and the large opening in the floor for cargo loading. The ladder at the back, near where the tail would be, gives access to the fuselage's upper deck. (Nicholas A Veronico)

The XC-99's starboard wing with three of the aircraft's six unique engine air intake scoops. The outer wing panels are not attached, and the lower fuselage lob can be seen on the left. (Jim Dunn)

Appendices

Appendix I

Inventory by Type (December 2020)

Type	Qty	Type	Qty	Type	Qty	Type	Qty
A-10A	49	E-2C	21	FA-18C	50	RF-8G	2
A-10C	51	E-3A	3	FA-18D	2	RH-53D	7
A-4E, F, M	11	E-8C	2	GA-10A	1	S-3A, B	93
A-6E	1	EA-6B	44	GR-7	3	SH-2F	26
AC-130H	6	EB-57B	5	GR-9	47	SH-3D, G, H	22
AC-130U	15	EC-130H	2	HC-130H	2	SH-60B, F	37
AH-1F, J, S,	23	EC-137D	1	HC-130N	7	SP-2H	1
AH-1W	101	EC-24A	1	HC-130P	17	T-1A	1
AT-38B	10	EP-3E	5	HH-1H, K	11	T-2B, C	67
AV-8B	8	ERA-3B	1	HH-46D	1	T-34C	233
B-1B	17	ES-3A	15	HH-60H	16	T-37B	80
B-52G	83	F-101B	1	KC-10A	3	T-38A	136
B-52H	12	F-105G	1	KC-130F, R, T	34	T-39D, E, G, N	37
B-57E	2	F-111F	1	KC-135D, E	105	T-43A	6
Boeing 707	1	F-14A	4	KC-135R	14	T-46A	1
BQM-34F	1	F-14B	2	LC-130F	4	TA-4B, F, J	60
C-130E	126	F-14D	3	MC-130E, H, P	37	TAV-8B	1
C-130H	62	F-15A	53	MH-53E, J, M	22	TC-12B	23
C-130J	1	F-15B	6	MH-60, R, S	12	TC-130H	1
C-131F	1	F-15C	93	MQ-1B	66	TC-18E, F	3
C-137B	4	F-15D	9	MQ-8B	2	TE-2C	1
C-145A	4	F-15E	1	NA-3B	1	TH-57A, D	7
C-20B, C, E, F	6	F-16A	201	NC-12B	1	TMK-12	8
C-20G, K	2	F-16B	37	NF-14A	1	TP-3A	4
C-21A	23	F-16C	112	NKC-135B, E	2	UC-12B	25
C-22A	1	F-16D	13	NP-3C, D	5	UH-1E, H, N, Y	68
C-23B, C, D	15	F3B	1	NT-39A	2	UP-3B	1
C-2A	5	F-4C	2	O-2A	7	US-2A	1
C-5A	57	F-4D	3	OΛ-4M	4	VH-34C	1
C-9A, B	20	F-4E	30	OV-1D	5	WB-57F	4
CH-46E	84	F-4F, J, S	20	P-3B	27	QC-130H	1
CH-53A, D	39	F-84F	1	P-3C	125	WC-135B, C	2
DC-130A	1	F-86F	1	QF-106A	1	XC-99	1
DC-9	4	FA-18A	57	RC-12F, M, N	7	YC-14	1
DHC-7	4	FA-18B	8	RF-4B, C	4	Total	3,220

Formerly a presidential fleet aircraft, VC-137B (707-153) 58-6971, *Freedom One*, served with the 89th Military Airlift Wing at Andrews AFB, Maryland, from 1959 until the type's replacement. This VC-137B returned the Iran hostages in 1981 and a decade later flew American POWs home from Operation *Desert Storm*. *Freedom One* was added to the Pima Collection on October 22, 1999. (Nicholas A Veronico)

Appendix II

The Pima Air and Space Museum

Do not miss the Pima Air and Space Museum, as it has acquired one of the world's most complete and diverse collections of commercial, fire bombing, and military aircraft in the western United States. Located adjacent to AMARG and Davis-Monthan AFB at 6000 E. Valencia Road, Tucson, visitors will see many aircraft that were formerly parked at the storage facility. The museum was founded in 1966 by a local coalition of Tucson aviation enthusiasts drawn from the community, its political leaders at all levels of government, the Air Force, and the Air Force Association. In October 1969, 35 aircraft from Celebrity Row were transferred to the museum to form the basis of the collection. The museum and its original collection of 48 aircraft formally opened to the public on May 8, 1976, and has never looked back!

Today there are more than 400 aircraft in the collection that range from World War Two-era bombers such as the B-17, B-24, and B-29; fighters like the P-51 Mustang, Supermarine Spitfire, Chance-Vought Corsair to the Century series of fighters – F-101, F-102, F-104, F-105, F-106; and the modern-era fleet like F-15s and F-16s, to the VC-118 used by Presidents Kennedy and Johnson, to the supersonic B-58 and SR-71. The Pima Air and Space Museum also has one of the world's largest collections of commercial aircraft, NASA aircraft, and an aerospace technology gallery. The museum features a restaurant and expertly curated museum store full of aerospace merchandise. All public areas of the facility have disabled access.

The Pima Air and Space Museum opened the Titan Missile Museum 25 miles south of Tucson (at 1580 W. Duval Mine Road, Sahuarita, Arizona), in May 1986. Tours of the former Titan II missile in its underground silo show the complex as it was when operated by the US Air Force's 390th Strategic Missile Wing. Visit the museum's website for tour times and prices.

Note: As of March 2020, the Pima Air and Space Museum is unable to provide tours of AMARG because of the Coronavirus quarantine. A decision on restarting AMARG bus tours has not been made at the time of writing. Should the tours not resume, it is anticipated that AMARG will provide a virtual tour accessible to everyone online.

Additional information, events, and a listing of Pima Air and Space Museum aircraft can be obtained at www.pimaair.org.

Dominating the outside display area is Convair B-36J 52-2827. Everything else looks small next to the Peacemaker. The aircraft is situated next to a B-47, a B-50, a trio of B-52s, and a B-58, for not only size comparison, but also to show the evolution of strategic bombers. (Nicholas A Veronico)

The 390th Bomb Group Memorial Museum is a "museum within a museum" as it is located on the grounds of the Pima Air and Space Museum. The 390th Memorial Museum pays tribute to men from the bomb group who served and sacrificed in the air war over Europe. The Lockheed/Vega-built B-17G 44-85828 has been painted to represent the 390th B-17 *I'll Be Around*. It is displayed next to a life-size mural of the crew positions (seen in the background). This museum is free to tour and is included in the Pima Air and Space Museum admission fee. (Jim Dunn)

Bibliography and Suggested Reading

Blanchard, Peter, Chinnery, Phillip and Swann, Martyn, *MASDC: Military Aircraft Storage & Disposition Center*, Aviation Press Ltd, London (1983)

Bonny, Danny, Fryer, Barry, and Swann, Martyn, *AMARC – Aerospace Maintenance & Regeneration Center, Davis-Monthan AFB, Arizona 1982–1997 (MASDC III)*, British Aviation Research Group, Surrey, England (2006)

Causey, Danny and Causey, Gregory, *Denizens of the Desert: AMARC Photographs by Danny Causey*, Romance Divine LLC (2008)

Chinnery, Philip D, *Desert Boneyard*, Airlife (England) (1987)

Chinnery, Philip D, *Boneyard Badges: Aircraft and Emblems at Davis-Monthan AFB*, Airlife (England) (2000)

Chinnery, Philip D, *50 Years of the Desert Boneyard*, Motorbooks International Co, Osceola, Wisconsin (1995)

Fryer, Barry and Swann, Martyn, *AMARC – Aerospace Maintenance & Regeneration Center, Davis-Monthan AFB, Arizona 1982–1997 (MASDC II)*, Aviation Press Ltd, London (1998)

Fugere, Jerry and Shane, Bob, *Inside AMARC: The Aerospace Maintenance and Regeneration Center, Tucson, Arizona*, MBI Publishing Co, St. Paul, Minnesota (2001)

Johnson, Dave, *The Aerospace Maintenance And Regeneration Center*, LAAS International, West Drayton, Middlesex, England (1995)

Kramer, Adel and Hoeveler, Patrick, *Desert Boneyards: Retired Aircraft Storage Facilities in the U.S*, Schiffer Military Publishing, Atglen, Pennsylvania (2010)

Larkins, William T, *Surplus WWII U.S. Aircraft*, BAC Publishers Inc, Upland, California (2005)

Laughery, Del, *Boneyard Almanac: The History and Current State of America's Largest Aircraft Collection*, CreateSpace Independent Publishing (2015)

Laughery, Del, *Boneyard Almanac: Aircraft Histories*, CreateSpace Independent Publishing (2015)

Laughery, Del, *Boneyard Almanac: Then and Now*, CreateSpace Independent Publishing (2017)

Laughery, Del, *Boneyard Almanac: 20th Century Picture Book*, CreateSpace Independent Publishing (2020)

Peake, William R, *McDonnell Douglas F-4 Phantom II: Production and Operational Data*, Midland Publishing, Hinckley, England (2004)

Scroggins III, James Douglas and Veronico, Nicholas A, *Junkyard Jets*, Stance and Speed, Minneapolis, Minnesota (2010)

Swann, Martyn, *309th AMARG (MASDC IV)*, British Aviation Research Group, Staffordshire, England (2013)

Swann, Martyn, *309th AMARG Revisited (MASDC V)*, British Aviation Research Group, Staffordshire, England (2017)

Veronico, Nicholas A, *Blue Angels: A Fly-By History: Sixty Years of Aerial Excellence*, Zenith Press, Osceloa, Wisconsin (2005)

Veronico, Nicholas A and Dunn, Jim, *Giant Cargo Planes*, MBI Publishing Co, Osceola, Wisconsin (1999)

Veronico, Nicholas A, Dunn, Jim and Strong, Ron, *Boneyard Nose Art: U.S. Military Aircraft Markings and Artwork*, Stackpole Books, Mechanicsburg, Pennsylvania (2013)

Veronico, Nicholas A, and Dunn, Jim, *21st Century U.S. Air Power*, MBI Publishing Co, St Paul, Minnesota (2004)

Veronico, Nicholas A, Grantham, A Kevin, and Thompson, Scott, *Military Aircraft Boneyards*, MBI Publishing Co, St Paul, Minnesota (2000)

Veronico, Nicholas A and Strong, Ron, *AMARG: America's Military Aircraft Boneyard*, Specialty Press, North Branch, Minnesota (2010)

Web Links
AMARC
The AMARC Experience: www.amarcexperience.com
Martyn Swann's AMARC website: www.amarc.info

Aircraft Types
Everything you need to know about C-130s: www.C-130.net
P-3 Orion Research Group, the Netherlands: www.p3Orion.nl
The Skyhawk Association: www.Skyhawk.org